Neural Networks in Organizational Research

Neural Networks in Organizational Research

Applying Pattern Recognition to the Analysis of Organizational Behavior

**David Scarborough
and Mark John Somers**

AMERICAN PSYCHOLOGICAL ASSOCIATION • WASHINGTON, DC

Published by
American Psychological Association
750 First Street, NE

Washington, DC 20002
www.apa.org

To order
APA Order Department
P.O. Box 92984
Washington, DC 20090-2984
Tel: (800) 374-2721
Direct: (202) 336-5510
Fax: (202) 336-5502
TDD/TTY: (202) 336-6123
Online: www.apa.org/books/
E-mail: order@apa.org

In the U.K., Europe, Africa, and the Middle East, copies may be ordered from
American Psychological Association
3 Henrietta Street
Covent Garden, London
WC2E 8LU England

Typeset in Goudy by World Composition Services, Inc., Sterling, VA

Printer: Edwards Brothers, Inc., Ann Arbor, MI
Cover Designer: Mercury Publishing Services, Rockville, MD
Technical/Production Editor: Tiffany L. Klaff

The opinions and statements published are the responsibility of the authors, and such opinions and statements do not necessarily represent the policies of the American Psychological Association.

Library of Congress Cataloging-in-Publication Data

Scarborough, David.
    Neural networks in organizational research : applying pattern recognition to the analysis of organizational behavior / David Scarborough & Mark John Somers.—1st ed.
        p. cm.
    Includes bibliographical references and index.
    ISBN 1-59147-415-9
    1. Organizational behavior—Research—Methodology. 2. Neural networks (Computer science) 3. Pattern perception. I. Somers, Mark John. II. Title.

HD58.7.S287   2006
302.3'50285632—dc22   2005036583

British Library Cataloguing-in-Publication Data
A CIP record is available from the British Library.

Printed in the United States of America
First Edition

CONTENTS

Foreword ix
G. *David Garson*

Acknowledgments xi

Introduction 3

I. Orientation 9

Chapter 1. Neural Networks in Organizational
            Research 11
            Why Use Neural Networks for Organizational
                Research? 13
            When Should Neural Networks Be Used? 14

Chapter 2. Science, Organizational Research, and
            Neural Networks 19
            Scientific Method and Empiricism 19
            The Role of Mathematics 20
            Behavioral Science 21
            Behavioral Research in Organizations 24
            Information Technology, Social Science, and
                Artificial Intelligence 26

Chapter 3. Neural Network Theory, History, and Concepts 29
            Early Theories 29
            Modern Theories of Neural Processes 30
            Innovation Drives Renewed Interest 37
            Backpropagation Neural Networks 38

A Taxonomy of Modern Artificial Neural
  Networks 40
Supervised Feed-Forward Neural Networks
  Described in This Book 42

Chapter 4.   Neural Networks as a Theory Development Tool 45
             Linearity, Neural Networks, and Organizational
               Research 46
             A Case for Nonlinearity in Organizational
               Research 47
             Neural Networks as a Theory Development Tool ... 48
             Using Artificial Neural Networks as an Exploratory
               Technique to Model the Job Satisfaction–Job
               Performance Relationship 52
             Neural Networks and Complexity Theory 56
             Artificial Neural Networks as a Force for
               Change in Organizational Research 57
             Neural Networks and Applied Research 58

Chapter 5.   Using Neural Networks in Organizational Research 61
             Getting Started: Factors to Consider in
               Evaluating Neural Network Software 62
             Getting Started: Choosing the Right
               Neural Network 67
             Unsupervised Neural Networks: Using
               Self-Organizing Maps 68
             Supervised Networks: Training Neural Networks
               for Prediction and Classification 71
             Neural Networks and Multivariate Statistics in
               Organizational Research 82
             Interpreting Neural Network Behavior
               Using Graphics 82

II. Applications 87

Chapter 6.   Statistics, Neural Networks, and
             Behavioral Research 89
             Neural Networks and Statistics 90
             Neural Networks and Behavioral Prediction in
               Organizations 94

Chapter 7.   Using Neural Networks in Employee Selection 101
             Scientific Employee Selection 102
             Statistical Models of Criterion Validity 103
             Neural Networks and Criterion Validation 104

Neural Validation Modeling 105
Why Use Neural Networks for Employee
    Selection? 105
Employee Selection Neural Networks 110

Chapter 8.   Using Self-Organizing Maps to Study
Organizational Commitment 123
Uncovering Patterns of Commitment With a
    Self-Organizing Map 124
Clustering Techniques for Deriving Commitment
    Profiles 126
The Study: Rationale and Variables 127
Overview of Methodology 128
Data Analysis: k-Means Clustering and
    Self-Organizing Maps 129
Findings: k-Means Versus Self-Organizing Map 129
Implications 130

III.   Implications 135

Chapter 9.   Limitations and Myths 137
Limitations of Neural Networks 137
Myths 141

Chapter 10.   Trends and Future Directions 145
Neural Networks and Behavioral Research in
    Organizations 146
Opportunities for New Research 153
Neural Network Applications 155

Appendix: Backpropagation Algorithm 159

Glossary 161

References 165

Index 177

About the Authors 187

FOREWORD

G. DAVID GARSON

In *Neural Networks in Organizational Research: Applying Pattern Recognition to the Analysis of Organizational Behavior*, David Scarborough and Mark John Somers have written a volume more useful than the larger number of "how-to" books that characterize neural network analysis texts. They have written a "why-to" book that provides the intellectual rationale for use of neural procedures by organizational and social scientists and that will contribute to the diffusion of this important methodology in related fields.

Perhaps because neural procedures are not based on the general linear model, maximum likelihood estimation, or other mainstays of traditional statistical analysis, they have not become embedded in the mandatory research training of the psychological and social sciences. However, Scarborough and Somers demonstrate how neural models can be used effectively to explore theoretical models and refine hypotheses. By focusing less on equations and derivations and more on the use of neural methods in what it is researchers actually do, the authors have written a highly accessible book, which is much needed in the field and may help make the case for bringing neural network analysis to the mainstream of methodological training for future generations of researchers.

Organizational researchers will particularly benefit by the later chapters of the book, which treat the modeling of employee selection and retention issues using neural backpropagation procedures and the modeling of employee commitment using neural self-organizing networks. More broadly, however, the authors perform a valuable service in earlier chapters by presenting the intellectual history of neural analysis, the range of organizational and other applications for neural methods, and the research issues and choices that the methodology involves.

A particular contribution of this volume is the focus on self-organizing neural networks as an alternative to traditional cluster analysis. Overcoming the popular view that equates neural network analysis with backpropagation modeling alone, Scarborough and Somers show neural network analysis to be not just a tool, but a toolkit capable of supporting a number of approaches. Self-organizing networks have received insufficient attention and the authors' presentation, which embeds it in theory development, is an important thrust of this work.

In their final chapter, Scarborough and Somers write, "As artificial neural networks become more widely accepted in organizational research, they have the potential to influence how research questions are framed, how theory is developed, and how research findings are interpreted and applied" (chap. 10, this volume, p. 145). The final chapter explores how and why this may come to pass. That neural network analysis has potential has been long known among the relatively small group of researchers who are familiar with its procedures. This volume serves the important function of articulating persuasively the potential role of neural methods in theory development in the social sciences.

ACKNOWLEDGMENTS

We would like to thank our editors at the American Psychological Association Books Department for their guidance and their patience. Also, the role of peer reviewer is often a thankless task. Earl Hunt (University of Washington), David Autor (MIT), and Charles Hulin (University of Illinois) contributed generously of their time and insight to help us refine the original manuscript. Scott Newbert, assistant professor of management at Villanova University, offered very helpful advice on the chapter on theory building, and we are very grateful. All errors, omissions, and mistakes that remain are solely ours.

I (Scarborough) would like to thank my wife Shelly and children Adam and Hollis for their loving support and patience through this and many other professional commitments that have taken from our time together. Also, my sincere gratitude goes to my colleagues at Unicru and the visionary client executives who have made this work possible.

I (Somers) would like to thank Bill Van Buskirk, former provost and distinguished professor at the New Jersey Institute of Technology, for allowing me to undertake this project while continuing as dean of the School of Management. I would also like to thank the doctoral faculty and students in business at Rutgers University for their helpful comments at a seminar I presented on neural networks.

Neural Networks in Organizational Research

INTRODUCTION

Today every major branch of the behavioral–social science collective offers specialized training in the study of human behavior in organizations. Industrial/organizational psychology, organizational sociology, labor economics, economic ethnography, human factors engineering, management, and related specialties share a common object of study. Perspectives, training, and theoretical approaches vary, but interdisciplinary borrowing of statistical techniques, measurement procedures, research design, and application of findings is well documented (Rappa & Debackere, 1992; Rucci & Tweney, 1980). Given the common object of study across these multiple disciplines, those who study human behavior in organizations cannot afford to be *method-centric*.[1] Nor should opportunistic awareness of method be limited to the behavioral sciences.

Artificial neural networks (ANNs) are the operationalized convergence of decades of research in information science, biology, statistics, electrical engineering, and other scientific disciplines. ANNs have been widely deployed in the physical sciences and used to solve many complex problems previously considered intractable. Today, ANNs are used in a wide array of pattern recognition, classification, simulation, and function optimization problems (Caudill & Butler, 1992; Garson, 1998; Haykin, 1999).

---

[1]**Method-centrism** *n*: An irrational bias favoring familiar methods or an unconsidered predisposition against unfamiliar methods (with apologies to *Webster's*).

3

Commercial applications include robotic vision and control systems; investment analysis and bankruptcy forecasting; economic policy simulation; credit card fraud detection; currency arbitrage; commodities trading; real-time process control in chemical and nuclear energy production; airline, train, and truck route optimization; automated telephone switching; voice and handwriting recognition; heating and air-conditioning climate control; and manufacturing production scheduling and quality control. Published government applications involving neural network technology include threat detection in airline luggage screening, missile guidance and flight control systems, and cryptographic analysis. Scientific and health care applications include spacecraft navigation, genome mapping, and medical diagnostics (Bylinsky, 1993; Garson, 1998; Glatzer, 1992; Haykin, 1999; Schwartz, 1992).

Prior to the mid-1990s, there was very little crossover between the major statistical software packages used by social scientists and software developed in fields associated with artificial intelligence. Artificial intelligence applications developed by scientists studying information theory, cybernetics, ANNs, robotics, expert systems, and fuzzy logic were generally not available or widely used by social scientists. Behavioral scientists experimenting with these procedures during that period were required to use software developed for engineering applications (Collins & Clark, 1993; Dickieson & Wilkins, 1992; Garson, 1991a) or develop their own software. This is no longer the case.

A review of the behavioral science literature reveals that in the past decade, research using neural network analysis has been applied to the prediction of child sexual abuse, white-collar crime, violent behavior, depression in adolescents, and recreational drug use. Furthermore, neural networks have been applied to psychiatric diagnosis and prognosis, combat psychology, test and construct validation, problem solving, identification of structure in personality data, modeling memory and amnesia, rule learning and memory encoding, music perception, natural language processing, and catastrophe analysis (Garson, 1998; Hanges, Lord, Godfrey, & Raver, 2002; Ostberg, 2005). The narrow focus of this book concerns the use of neural networks as a class of analytic procedures applied to behavioral research in organizations.

Artificial neural networks are used to reveal and model patterns in data. As with other analytic procedures operationalized in software, effective use requires some understanding of the underlying concepts and processes. Academics and practitioners interested in using neural networks in organizational research will find it necessary to think differently about how they approach data analysis and about the interpretation of findings. Although ANNs represent a clear break from more conventional analyses, there are analogs to concepts from the general linear model (see Somers, 1999). We, of course, point those out whenever possible to orient the reader and to help facilitate the transition into the world of neural computing. Last, we feel that it is important to emphasize that one does not have to be a programmer or an expert in artificial intelligence to use neural networks effectively.

The primary objective of this book is to provide a practical, step-by-step approach to using neural networks in organizational research. It is written for graduate students and practitioners who have some familiarity with multivariate statistics and statistical software. In thinking about how we might meet this objective, several things became clear (perhaps not as quickly as we or APA Books would have liked). First, it is important to provide a clear and accessible explanation of what neural networks are and how they work. Second, neural networks must be explained within the context of organizational research and tied to theory building and theory testing. Without this piece of the puzzle, one is left with a "cookbook" approach to using ANNs that is not likely to attract many "chefs." Third, it is necessary to demonstrate applications of neural networks to problems of interest to organizational psychologists and other researchers with real data and real results. Finally, we think it is important to give readers a clear idea of the limitations of neural networks and a sense of how they might influence organizational research in the future.

David Scarborough and Mark John Somers have used neural networks for quite some time, the former in academic and applied research, and the latter in academic research. It is clear that we possess an enthusiasm for the promise of ANNs in organizational research and would like to see that promise come to fruition. That having been said, we have taken great care to avoid "overselling" neural networks to scholars and practitioners (several reviewers were very helpful in this regard, and we are grateful for their astute comments).

The book is divided into three parts: orientation, applications, and implications. Chapter 1 defines neural networks as a class of statistical procedures and suggests guidelines for deciding when they might be useful. The next two chapters provide a brief summary of the scientific and historic context of organizational science and neural network theory. Chapter 2 is written for those who may wish to review the scientific method, empirical formalism, and organizational research. The evolution of neural network theory and a general taxonomy of neural networks are presented in chapter 3. Many readers may find this review interesting whereas others may wish to skip forward selectively.

Introductory material aside, chapter 4 presents the case for using neural networks to improve, test, and refine our theories of organizational behavior. Chapter 5 is a general introduction to neural modeling. It begins with choosing software and neural network paradigms appropriate for different kinds of research problems. The parameters of neural network development are defined in the context of their statistical corollaries; and the basics of training, testing, and evaluating neural networks and their output are covered.

The applications section of the book begins in chapter 6 with a review of the literature describing published and unpublished research on the use of ANNs in the behavioral sciences. Chapter 7 describes the use of one class of neural networks (trained feed-forward networks) to model predictive relationships in employment data for employee selection decision support. Chapter 8 covers the application of another type of network (self-organizing maps) for exploring organizational commitment profiles obtained from survey data.

The final two chapters of the book describe the limitations of neural network analysis and provide additional guidelines for determining when the use of neural networks makes sense. Chapter 10 attempts to bring the various threads of reasoning presented throughout the book to a unified theme—that ANNs are practical pattern recognition tools that are being productively used in all scientific disciplines, including behavioral research in organizations. The book concludes with some reasonable speculation about the kinds of research applications that extend the logic of pattern recognition problem solving.

As the use of neural networks in behavioral research becomes more common, the advantages and limitations of these procedures will be further documented, debated, and refined. We are convinced that neural network analysis will become a standard component of behavioral science analysis. A growing body of evidence suggests that neural networks can enhance the use of, and in some applications, replace conventional multivariate procedures in academic and applied research.

Massive computation speed and memory allow computers to represent symbolic information in ways that human minds can conceive but not duplicate. Human brains can only hold three to seven objects in consciousness simultaneously, and humans experience time as a linear progression. As a result, humans have become particularly adept at sequential processing, induction, and deduction. This innate cognitive and perceptual filter is reflected in scientists' search for simple axioms that explain their experiences, their preference for sequential formulaic representation of truth, and their constant attempts to generalize what they have learned and predict what will happen next.

In contrast to human capacities, active computer memory is vast, limited only by expandable hardware parameters, software efficiency, and the bit requirements of object representation. The capacity to hold many multidimensional objects, states, and processes in active memory allows synthetic intelligence to apprehend great complexity. Apprehension, however, does not imply understanding. Comprehension, in the sense of interpretation, evaluation, and assignment of meaning, remains the duty of the human tool user. Our challenge is to understand how machine intelligence differs from our own and, through that understanding, learn to use these remarkable new tools effectively.

I
ORIENTATION

1

NEURAL NETWORKS IN
ORGANIZATIONAL RESEARCH

Behavioral scientists working in organizations today have access to unprecedented amounts of data. Networked computing and software tools are changing the landscape of organizational research in fundamental ways. Information technology facilitates creation of vast amounts of data. In organizational research, online surveys, interactive interviews, computer-based assessment, and other digital tools have become a preferred medium for collecting self-report and opinion data. Political polling, marketing surveys, employee selection and placement, educational assessment, and other kinds of research can be completed faster than ever at a lower cost with targeted access to specific populations. Because source data are entered directly into the medium of analysis, transaction costs of electronic data collection have declined while data quality and yield have increased as user-interface design has improved (Howell, 1991).

Other unobtrusive, nontraditional sources of behavioral observation data are coming into use. Measures of online behavior and databases maintained by corporations and government agencies for other purposes can be a useful source of research data. Small sample size, a primary source of error in social research, is less of a problem for researchers working with online data sources.

Concurrent with expanding data availability, analytic capability and processing capacity have improved dramatically. New and better statistical software has evolved to accommodate the needs of researchers challenged by vast data resources. One permutation of this evolution is the recent appearance of computationally intensive methods only recently enabled by spectacular gains in processing speed. These "brute force" computational techniques were often developed to solve highly complex problems in the physical sciences and are now migrating into the toolkit of organizational research. Artificial neural networks constitute one class of these powerful new tools.

An artificial neural network (ANN) is a statistical model comprised of simple, interconnected processing elements that are configured through iterative exposure to sample data. Artificial neural networks were originally developed as mathematical theories of the information-processing activity of biological nerve cells. As a result of this history, the structural elements and vocabulary used to describe ANNs have conceptual analogs from neuroscience[1] despite their general acceptance as a class of statistical procedures. A summary of this history is presented in chapter 3.

Continuing briefly with the biology metaphor, ANNs form internal representations (mathematical models) of the external world (a sampled function) in response to exposure to stimuli (sample data). Artificial neural networks "learn" in the same sense that a fitted regression equation has "learned" a sampled function. Through multiple exposures to sample data, structural elements within the network are reconfigured to approximate distributions, associations, and other features of the data.

Like a fitted regression function, a trained neural network can generalize pattern information (apply learning) to new data. For example, a neural network trained with assessment responses and job performance measures from an employee sample can be used to estimate the job performance of applicants on the basis of their responses to the same assessment. In that application, neural network output is interpreted as the test score just as with a regression scoring model.

Perhaps the most significant difference between neural and statistical modeling is the method used to derive the functional model. The statistician predefines, iteratively tests, and selects the best of the hypothesized objective functions to derive a final model. Developing a neural model involves preparing data for presentation to the network, selecting a training regime (the learning rule), configuring the initial layout of neurons (the network architecture), and then monitoring training progress until a satisfactory model converges. This is always an iterative process in which results from successive training cycles inform modifications to the network or the training

---

[1] Examples of biological nomenclature inherent to neural network analysis include labeling processing elements as "neurons" and describing the algorithms used to update connections between neurons as "learning rules."

regime while repeating the process. Heuristics for these procedures are described in chapter 5. Experienced statisticians may wonder why one would go to such trouble.

WHY USE NEURAL NETWORKS FOR ORGANIZATIONAL RESEARCH?

To answer this question, the following discussion draws from the experience of other disciplines that have adopted neural network modeling procedures, as well as research by behavioral scientists working with ANNs in academia and organizations. ANNs have advantages for solving certain kinds of research problems. In addition, ANNs have other properties that support their use in applied research, as discussed in the following sections.

The most significant departure of neural network analysis from conventional analysis is that neural model development is relatively unconstrained by researcher expectations compared with the defined parameters of anticipated functional relationships inherent to hypothesis testing. Neural network analysis does not require or yield individual hypothesis confirmation. A trained neural network's output and structure are used to make inferences about associations, interactions, nonlinearities, and other characteristics of the data. If such inferences are accurate, they can be replicated across multiple networks and samples and confirmed using conventional procedures. The important point here is that ANNs can help us uncover structural elements in research data that we may not have known of or thought to look for. This includes surfacing meaningful relationships in addition to spurious ones. Discerning useful and theoretically meaningful network behavior from sample-specific noise is one of the challenges of neural analysis. Fortunately, conventional modeling procedures, sampling strategies, and heuristics specific to neural modeling are available for interpreting neural network output and behavior.

Even though the neural modeling approach does not require theoretical specification, the use of any general function simulator[2] for behavioral analysis and prediction increases the need for a coherent theoretical approach and rigorous methodology. Knowledge of likely predictive associations, reliable construct measurement and scaling, preanalytic power analysis, and other features of well-structured research are just as critical to neural model development as they are to conventional modeling.

---

[2] Artificial neural networks are one of several different curve-fitting procedures including polynomial regression, multiple regression splines, neuro-fuzzy inference systems, genetic algorithms, and radial basis functions (Friedman, 1991; Hastie, Tibshirani, & Friedman, 2001; Westbury, Buchanan, Sanderson, Rhemtulla, & Phillips, 2003).

WHEN SHOULD NEURAL NETWORKS BE USED?

Themes introduced in the following paragraphs are discussed in more detail in later chapters. They are presented here to introduce a rationale for using ANNs and the conditions under which they are most likely to add value to a research project. Considerations for applying ANNs in theoretical research are followed by a discussion of factors related to operational use of ANNs. In general, when one or more of the following conditions are present in a research project, neural network analysis may have value in concert with or even in lieu of conventional multivariate analysis.

When sample data show high dimensionality, multiple variable types, and complex interaction effects or do not meet parametric assumptions

ANNs are nonparametric function simulators. Unlike modeling procedures derived from the general linear model, ANNs can be used to model data sets that would otherwise violate statistical assumptions of normality or linearity. Assuming sufficient sampling and proper training, ANNs will fit a sampled distribution accurately and are thus useful for modeling data with unknown distributional characteristics (Walker & Milne, 2005). ANNs do not require independence among variables and will model significant interactions between variables. This characteristic of ANNs is discussed further in chapter 3, which introduces the mathematics of backpropagation training and explains how neural networks map relationships in sample data using gradient descent optimization.[3]

When evaluation of alternative models is required

Artificial neural networks can provide a useful benchmark for evaluating other types of models, linear or nonlinear. Most neural network software programs include utilities for scaling, data cleansing, feature selection, and automated model creation and testing. These tools allow researchers to efficiently create families or *ensembles* of neural networks that vary by architecture, learning rule, convergence conditions, and other parameters. This type of brute force computational attack can provide reasonable initial estimates of model fit that might be obtained using other modeling approaches on a given data set. Other information on the extent of nonlinearity, interactions, and generalizability can be gleaned as well.

In addition to exploratory estimates of model fit, the performance of optimized neural models can be compared directly with that of conventional

---

[3] Backpropagation is the process by which error values (the difference between predicted and actual outcomes) are used to modify the connections between neurons in training neural networks. It is the most commonly used ANN gradient descent algorithm and one of many computational approaches to minimizing error between a function approximation and sample data (Kosko, 1992).

models. In many instances, a fully specified conventional model that maps the underlying function to a theory-based explanation is required. If neural model fit is significantly better than that of the specified model, this may indicate that the model is incomplete or that some functional relationships are not being represented accurately. The model fit of an optimized neural network that generalizes to independent data reliably can be viewed as a reasonable approximation of the explainable variance in a data set. When a specified formal model approximates the fit of an optimized neural network (or better, an ensemble of neural networks), this can be viewed as one form of corroboration of the specified model. Chapter 6 provides a review of the literature of research comparing ANNs with familiar multivariate procedures in organizational research.

When relationships between independent and dependent variables are weak and unexplained variance is large

Behavioral scientists have access to a wide range of tools for measuring attitudes, beliefs, traits, abilities, preferences, and other individual differences that have utility for theory development and testing, behavioral prediction, program evaluation, population segmentation, and other research objectives. In chapter 4, we discuss low effect size and poor model fit as possible symptoms of the limitations and unquestioned assumptions inherent to commonly used multivariate methods. Artificial neural networks complement existing methods by improving detection and description of nonlinearities, interaction effects, and other complexities in sample data. As such, ANNs have a useful role to play in theory testing and refinement.

When the research application supports or requires the use of data-mining procedures

In applied settings, data mining is the growing practice of applying exploratory and confirmatory analysis to large-scale databases to uncover useful relationships embedded therein (Ye, 2003). In chapter 7, the use of criterion valid employee selection models developed using data sources created for other purposes is described. Cost-efficient predictor content can be derived from employment applications and assessment records collected via computer networks. On the criterion side, payroll data containing length of service, termination records, promotion or demotion activity, compensation changes, and other data can be scaled to reflect meaningful performance differences among workers. Other potentially useful sources of performance criteria include records of sales and commission data, unit production, service transactions, accidents and disciplinary records, performance appraisal ratings, and other quantifiable measures of job performance that can be linked to specific employees for whom matching predictor data are available.

In data mining, very large sample size and very low data acquisition costs are offset by variable data integrity and little experimental control over data collection. Opportunistic data mining is a scavenger's game, and numerous caveats apply. Careful examination and preprocessing of opportunistic validation data should precede any attempt at modeling. Feature selection, choosing the right set of predictor variables, is challenging because such data were collected for purposes other than behavioral research. In this type of validation project, characterized by large sample size, noisy predictor and criterion data, minimal theoretical grounding, limited experimental control, and exclusively electronic model processing, a neural network may be the only viable modeling choice.

When the theoretical basis of prediction is ambiguous or poorly understood

In employee selection research, some criterion valid predictors of job effectiveness are based on scientific theories that are still evolving. A good example of this is the use of standardized measures of biographical facts related to life history, work experience, and so on, often referred to as *biodata* (Nickels, 1994). Well-designed biodata predictors can provide robust prediction when validated locally but often do not generalize across multiple work settings, even for similar jobs. Several competing theories have been advanced to explain biodata validity and utility; however, the generalizability problem remains the subject of ongoing debate and research (Mumford, Snell, & Reiter-Palmon, 1994). Ambiguity or absence of a sound theoretical model explaining how and why a predictor set should relate to available criterion measures is, in our opinion, a reasonable methodological justification for applying a neural modeling procedure.

When operational use of the predictive model requires high fault tolerance

Electronic survey data collection is administered by software controls and user-interface design instead of human proctors. The loss of environmental control over unproctored completion of electronic questionnaires simultaneously increases sample size and response pattern variation. Internet applicant populations are in theory unlimited by geographic constraints and show wider linguistic and cultural variation. Differences in education, motivation, reading ability, computing dexterity, and many other factors contribute to response variability. Additional threats to data integrity are inherent to the computer medium. Software glitches, hardware failures, network traffic, and other factors can degrade digital data and further increase the variability of applicant data from online sources.

In chapter 6 the findings of Collins and Clark (1993); Garson (1991a); and Stanton, Sederburg, and Smith (2000) are described in which data integrity was systematically degraded to compare performance decline between various neural networks and a variety of statistical models. The ability of neural networks to produce reasonable estimates using noisy and missing input variables is a significant advantage over more brittle[4] modeling procedures for processing complex unrefined data of variable quality in real-time applications.

High fault tolerance and graceful degradation of model accuracy are two properties of neural network models that have speeded their deployment in various engineering applications with high noise input data. Nuclear energy production, refinery control systems, voice and image recognition, and signal processing involving large-dimension, nonlinear, complex streaming data sources were among the first neural network applications (Caudill & Butler, 1992; Glatzer, 1992; Schwartz, 1992). In our opinion, a similar technology transfer will occur in real-time processing of behavioral data. Criterion valid neural models in operational use for online employee selection systems are described in chapter 7.

When conventional modeling is unnecessary or cannot be completed under operational time constraints

We anticipate organizational research applications in which speed of model development will become a competitive or security advantage. In such applications, rapid deployment of generalized prediction or classification has priority over the need to specify and explain the objective function. ANN procedures developed to detect fraudulent credit card activity have been deployed in proprietary applications to detect transaction patterns associated with employee theft on point-of-sale systems. These and other potential applications of neural network techniques are discussed in chapter 10.

---

[4]Brittleness refers to the fault tolerance of a predictive model. Multivariate regression, discriminant, and quadratic model accuracy degrades rapidly or fails when one or more independent variables presented to the model is noise (e.g., a missing value or a random value of unexpected magnitude or valence). Neural networks encode functional relationships across a dispersed connection weight matrix. The effects of missing or unexpected input variables are dispersed within the network, causing degradation of model performance without catastrophic failure.

2

SCIENCE, ORGANIZATIONAL RESEARCH, AND NEURAL NETWORKS

This chapter provides a brief historical perspective on the scientific method and the evolution of mathematics and technology. The social and behavioral sciences have distinct challenges not shared with the physical sciences. These issues are presented, followed by a discussion of advantages and responsibilities shared by all scientists enabled with modern computers. Awareness of our scientific heritage provides a useful starting point for understanding the context of organizational research.

SCIENTIFIC METHOD AND EMPIRICISM

The scientific method of knowledge discovery is to observe and measure a phenomenon, develop a theory that explains observations, and then test the accuracy of the theory through systematic experimentation. As this process is repeated, the measurements and theories are refined, modified, or rejected as experimental results are interpreted and used to develop better measures, theories, and new experiments. A defining aspect of the scientific method requires that the observations, measurements, theories, and experiments be specified and quantified in a manner that allows independent verification of results.

As the cycle of observation, measurement, hypothesis formation, and testing is repeated, cumulative scientific understanding is expressed and reexpressed using formalized theories and models. Formalization refers to mathematical specification or the practice of summarizing scientific insight using formulaic representation. In this way, scientists share current understanding and interpretation of observations, measures, and experiments using the concise precision of modern mathematics. Albert Einstein gave one of the best definitions:

> Science is the attempt to make the chaotic diversity of sense-experience correspond to a logically uniform system of thought. In this system, single experiences must be correlated with the theoretic structure in such a way that the resulting coordination is unique and convincing. (Einstein, 1940, p. 323)

THE ROLE OF MATHEMATICS

In terms of affecting human history, the discovery that symbolic logical systems can be used to represent relationships, processes, and events in the physical world is comparable with the evolution of language, the discovery of fire, the invention of agriculture, and written history. The symbiotic evolution and differentiation of mathematical systems and their technological expression continue to transform human life and civilization. The history of science and technology is inextricably bound to the history of mathematics.

The extraordinary gains in science that followed Newtonian physics reinforced the growing acceptance of logical positivism as the philosophical foundation of science. Logical positivism or empiricism emerged from the writings of Kepler, Galileo, Descartes, Kant, and many others who rejected the Aristotelian idea that reason alone was sufficient for the discernment of truth. The comments of others are illustrative:

> In any scientific or technological field, such as astronomy, chemistry, engineering, physics, etc., the formulation of a natural law is regarded as completely precise and definitive only when it is expressed as a mathematical equation. (Sturt, 1923, p. 70)

> The logical positivist position is embodied in what has come to be called "the verifiability theory of meaning." As its proponents have pointed out, it is better construed, not as a theory, but as a rule or methodological norm. Loosely, it prescribes that a statement is to be taken as meaningful only if it is capable of empirical verification and its meaning is the mode of its verification. (Kaplan, 1964, p. 36)

> Logical positivism holds that if you cannot test or mathematically prove what you say, you have said nothing. (Kosko, 1993, p. 71)

After Newton and to this day, the precepts of empiricism and the scientific method remain the fundamental currency of research and knowledge discovery in mainstream science. Contributions to the fund of scientific knowledge are expressed, shared, evaluated, and advanced within this philosophical and logical framework.

Throughout the history of science, the discovery or invention of a mathematical model that was isomorphic with observed phenomena was often followed by application and refinement of the new analytic method by other scientists. Incremental evolution in mathematical representation has advanced both scientific understanding and technological progress, opening new avenues of discovery. In this sense, the history of science is the history of man's ability to represent observed reality within the structure of a system of numeric representation.

If a formal model accurately represents the salient characteristics of a theory and that theory explains a particular phenomenon, scientists can extrapolate unknown facts about the phenomenon by observing what should happen according to the theoretical model. Thus scientists attempt to deduce from observation the underlying structure or principles that would explain their measurements. Informed by explanatory models, scientists make educated guesses about future events or the results of experiments with varying degrees of certainty. To the extent that experimental and theoretical results consistently agree, theoretical principles are supported or rejected.

BEHAVIORAL SCIENCE

When an astronomer forecasts the arrival of a cyclic asteroid many years in the future, we would be surprised if the space rock did not arrive at the appointed hour. If a chemist found the atomic weight of a new compound to be different from the predicted value, she would assume that a procedural error in the lab caused the variance rather than question the mathematical model of the underlying chemical reaction. Astronomy and chemical engineering have evolved sophisticated explanatory models that describe the behavior and structure of physical processes with a very high degree of accuracy.

This is not true of the social sciences in which the object of study is human behavior. Explanatory and predictive theoretical models in the social sciences are several orders of magnitude less accurate than models of the physical world. Scientific research in organizations, a subset of the larger domain of the behavioral sciences, is no exception. This is not to say that behavioral science has not advanced since the time of Francis Galton, Francis Edgeworth, Karl Pearson, and other founders. However, behavioral science has not developed formal theories that permit explanation and prediction at the level achieved by 17th-century physics.

To understand why this is, it is useful to acknowledge the special challenges facing behavioral scientists that are not shared by physical scientists. First, the physical manifestation of behavior is difficult to link to causal processes occurring within the organism. Behavioral measurement in animal and human subjects, even when tightly framed, is analyzed and interpreted using attribution and reconstruction to infer objective facts about opaque inner processes that are not directly observable. Second, behavior is a time-bound, dynamic phenomenon that is measured using operationalized constructions of concepts describing the object of study. In addition to measurement and methodological challenges, the origins and expressions of behavior are complex and inherently problematic for representation using formulaic reduction in the classic tradition of scientific parsimony. Let us consider each special challenge in more detail.

Causes of Behavior Are Not Directly Observable

Mammalian nervous systems are among the most complicated structures found in nature. Neural biology reveals that the behavior of a single nerve cell is a highly complex interaction between the chemical and electrical microenvironment. Temporal and amplitude stimulus variation from other nerve cells, genetic and functionally determined structural constraints, and other factors influence neural activity.

A human brain is made up of about one hundred billion individual neurons (Williams & Herrup, 1988). Depending on function and learning, individual nerve cells may connect and interact with hundreds, even thousands of neighboring cells. In addition, neurons are differentiated to perform specific complex tasks, including perception, cognition, memory, emotion, voluntary and involuntary motor control, chemical and autonomic process regulation, and other tasks. Finally, brain cells change throughout the life span in response to learning, hormonal changes, environmental conditions, illness, nutrition, aging, and other factors.

Recent advances in brain imaging technology are beginning to unlock the physiological manifestation of neuropsychological events. Today, distinct cognitive activity can be measured in time to within a few milliseconds and spatially to within a few cubic millimeters (Hunt, 2002). Nevertheless, until real-time measurement of brain activity becomes significantly more capable, the study of human behavior is limited to measurement of the extrinsic features of multiple, complex intrinsic processes.

Behavior Is Transient and Difficult to Measure Reliably

Scientific observation of behavior occurs within specific historic and social contexts. The scientist–observer of human behavior, being human, is subject to a host of perceptual distortions that can and do influence what we study, how we study it, how we interpret our measurements, and how we extract meaning and theory from our observations. The boundaries between the causes and effects of behavior are difficult to distinguish; furthermore, scientific observation of behavior changes behavior.

When a scientist observes the behavior of a research subject, even unobtrusively, it is difficult to ascertain if that behavior would have occurred in nature and if the observer's interpretation of subject behavior is without perceptual bias. A strong case can be made for extending Heisenberg's famous uncertainty principle to the observation of human behavior. As experimental control increases, one's confidence in the independence of behavioral measures from observational effects invariably decreases.

Finally, behavior (especially human behavior) is highly complex. Genetic endowment, health, developmental stage, and other intrapersonal factors interact with environment to create wide behavioral variation in the same person. As one moves beyond the study of individuals to consider group behavior, the complexity of measurement and sources of error increase exponentially. Applied social scientists, organizational researchers included, can never eliminate or control for all sources of uncontrolled variation. Unlike the physical scientist, there is no readily observable theoretical verification of the behavioral scientist's observations and predictions. Instead, we must make inferences about human behavior in the context of the statistical apparatus that defines both our questions and the answers we obtain.

Early investigators of psychophysics addressed some of these complexities by adopting and refining statistical methods originally developed by astronomers to explain variations in celestial measurements across different observers of the same events. By the end of the 18th century, a theory of measurement error attributed to Gauss (observation = truth + error) allowed astronomers to use averaged estimates of expected values and probability distributions of error to verify Newtonian principles (Stigler, 1999). Having formal theory that defined the object of inference independently of observed measurement was an advantage not shared by scientists studying human behavior.

To measure phenomena that are not directly observable, early psychologists applied experimental design to manipulate conditions, establish baseline measures, and test hypotheses, thereby creating their object of inference using carefully structured experiments. Social scientists, lacking even experimental control over the conditions of measurement, were required to go further. For Edgeworth, Pearson, George Yule, and those who followed, the statistical model itself defined the object of inference, often a set of conditional expectations with given covariates. Fitting a distribution of measurements and defining the object of inference in terms of the constants observed allowed testing of conditional expectations against other measured characteristics. Historian Stephen Stigler (1999) observed,

> The role of statistics in social science is thus fundamentally different from its role in much of physical science, in that it creates and defines the objects of study much more directly. Those objects are no less real than those of physical science. They are even often much better understood . . . the same methods are useful in all areas. (p. 199)

Over the decades, measurement procedures, research design, and analytic methods in the social sciences have evolved significantly. As with other branches of science, specialization has led to differentiation as groups of scientists studying different aspects of human behavior developed divergent literature, methods, and statistics appropriate to different facets of human behavior. Throughout this journey, statistical procedures developed in the ranks of one discipline have been successfully adapted and used by scientists in other fields. The process of knowledge diffusion across scientific disciplines facilitates innovation as techniques developed for one purpose are applied to similar problems in other domains. Interdisciplinary awareness is particularly important and appropriate for those who study human behavior in organizations.

BEHAVIORAL RESEARCH IN ORGANIZATIONS

According to *Webster's Third New International Dictionary of the English Language*, *behavioral science* is the study of human action, whereas *social science* is the study of human relationships.

behavioral science n: a science (as psychology, sociology, anthropology) dealing with human action and aiming at the establishment of generalizations of man's behavior in society—compare SOCIAL SCIENCE.

social science n: the branches of science that deal with the institutions and functioning of human society and the interpersonal relationships of individuals as members of society **2**: a science (as economics or political science) dealing with a particular phase or aspect of human society—compare BEHAVIORAL SCIENCE.

These phrases are often used interchangeably, and indeed, definitions of both reference the other as an aid to understanding. The reason for this correspondence is simple. It is theoretically difficult, if not practically impossible, to observe behavior in a manner that is independent of social context. Likewise, measurement of human relationships without referencing behavior is meaningless. Finally, a third definition is offered.

organization *n*: . . . **2**: something organized: **a**: an organic being or system: organism **b**: a group of people that has a more or less constant membership, a body of officers, a purpose, and usu. a set of regulations . . . **3**: **a**: a state or manner of being organized: organic structure: purposive systematic arrangement: constitution: specifically: the administrative and functional structure of an organization (as a business, political party, military unit) including the established relationships of personnel through lines of authority and responsibility with delegated and assigned duties.

An organization is a group of people who interact and collectively behave in ways that serve a common purpose. Not surprisingly, social science vocabulary and concepts are embedded in this definition.

A recent review of the history of research methods in the field of industrial/organizational (I/O) psychology identifies three periods of development characterized by *establishment* (prior to 1936), *expansion* (1936–1969), and, from 1969 to 2000, *eutrophication* (Austin, Scherbaum, & Mahlman, 2002). The establishment of I/O psychology as a distinct specialty diverging from general and experimental psychology occurred prior to World War II. As the industrial revolution rolled across Western Europe and the United States, empirical study of behavior in organizations was described as early as the 1880s. The efficiencies of production introduced by Frederick Taylor's methods of worker time and motion optimization established the economic significance of the human element of production and the value of systematic experimentation with job duties and workers.

Management acceptance and support of Taylor's scientific management methods would open opportunities for Hugo Munsterberg, Robert Yerkes, and other psychologists to apply classical test theory and methods of psychometric measurement of individual differences to common problems of worker and soldier selection and placement (Munsterberg, 1913; Scott, 1911/1969; Yerkes, 1921). The first issue of the *Journal of Applied Psychology* was published in 1917. I/O research of the period consisted largely of descriptive and correlation studies in employment settings.

From 1936 to 1968, the field expanded as formal training programs multiplied, the subspecialty of organizational psychology emerged, and separate career paths for scientists working in academic and applied practice diverged as demand for behavioral research in organizations grew. New measurement procedures and concepts that came into use during this period include item response theory, construct validity, sampling theory, significance testing, and utility analysis. Many of today's commonly used statistical procedures emerged, notably the many variations on the general linear model (univariate and multivariate analysis of variance and covariance, canonical correlation, discriminant analysis, multivariate multiple regression). Multidimensional scaling, clustering procedures, power analysis, and nonparametric measures for association and independence appeared. Exploratory factor analysis became particularly prominent in I/O research during this period.

In recent years, research design, measurement procedures, and analytic methods in I/O psychology have reached new levels of complexity and sophistication. Austin et al. (2002) used the metaphor of eutrophication or ferment to characterize the state of the discipline from 1969 to 2000. The availability of a large complement of highly specialized and powerful techniques has made it more difficult for managers and other non-I/O psychologists (our traditional users and sponsors) to understand and evaluate I/O research. It is not coincidental that misuse of I/O methods has increased, and the field is littered with "unfinished innovations." Item response and generalizability theories are cited as exemplars of sound theoretical methodologies that have yet to be widely applied.

Perhaps the single most important source of innovation in recent decades for organizational research stems from the assimilation of information technology. Inexpensive real-time data collection and storage, global connectivity, and massive computational capacity are relatively new developments on the timeline of social science. A brief discussion of information science provides context for the use of neural networks in organizational research.

INFORMATION TECHNOLOGY, SOCIAL SCIENCE, AND ARTIFICIAL INTELLIGENCE

The first computers were human (Bailey, 1996). Until the middle of the 20th century, "computer" was a job title. Computers worked with scientists, actuaries, engineers, and the military performing arithmetic. An entry-level computer's position was similar in pay and occupational status to that of bookkeeper, stenographer, and other skilled clerical occupations. Senior-level computers were highly skilled mathematicians and included Adrien Legendre, who first described the method of least squares in 1805 (Stigler, 1999). The U.S. Ballistics Research Lab employed over 200 full-time computers during World War II.

Human computers were slow and made many errors. Efforts to automate sequential calculation appeared in the early 1800s with the work of Charles Babbage, Ada Lovelace, John Couch Adams, and others (Bailey, 1996). By the 1930s, the U.S. War Department had funded production of the first truly digital computer, which was designed to solve differential equations of ballistic trajectories. The Electronic Numerical Integrator and Calculator (ENIAC) contained 18,000 to 19,000 vacuum tubes, weighed 30 tons, and required floor space equal to about half of a basketball court. The machine could process positive and negative numbers, compare quantities, perform arithmetic, and extract square roots. ENIAC could perform about 5,000 floating point operations per second (for instance, adding, subtracting, or multiplying two numbers) and was a thousand times faster than previous analog machines using mechanical relays (Crevier, 1993). At the time, it took 20 hours for a skilled human computer using a desk calculator to calculate a 60-second trajectory. ENIAC took 30 seconds.

As computer hardware improved, demand for algorithms of coded instructions for computer problem solving gave rise to a new scientific profession: software engineering. As computers progressed from tubes to transistors and then to integrated circuits, software engineering evolved to improve the interface between human users and computers. Programming languages came to resemble natural language more closely. Then programs that write and execute lower level programs in response to real-time user input evolved. The graphic user interface (GUI) was invented at Xerox in the 1950s and allowed almost anyone to compose and execute computer instructions. By the early 1980s, today's mass market for personal computers was born.

Long before the personal computer (PC) revolution, large-scale mainframe computers had become the workhorse of information processing in government, business, and education. Many of these institutions, corporations, and agencies had developed an interconnected global network of computers used by scientists and officials worldwide to exchange data, send and receive messages, and publish findings. By the late 1980s, PCs began accessing the Internet, which evolved to accommodate noninstitutional computer users. At the turn of the millennium, the use of networked computers had become a common feature of work and private life in the industrialized nations and continues to expand to all regions of the world.

This brief history of computing is presented to illustrate how much the performance of modern computers has improved in the past half century. The use of floating point operations per second (flops) is only one metric of this performance, but it is illustrative of the direction and magnitude of the trend. Recall that ENIAC, at 5,000 flops, could perform in 30 seconds the equivalent of 20 hours of human computational effort, a 2,400% improvement. The performance of high-end desktop computers in 2005 is measured in gigaflops (billions of flops) with figures on current hardware in the range of 5 to 15 gigaflops. Using the median value, the performance of the contemporary machine is 2,000,000% better than ENIAC! The performance of today's supercomputers using parallel architectures is measured in teraflops (trillions of operations per second). Such computational power allows modern scientists to analyze in seconds problems that would have taken the U.S. Ballistics Research Lab of 1940 thousands of man-years to complete.

Working scientists today have advantages and tools that are historically unprecedented. Some of these tools have come from the convergence of research from different scientific disciplines. Artificial neural networks are one of these.

Artificial or machine intelligence is a specialized field of computer science that attempts to simulate human and other forms of intelligence with computer circuits and sophisticated software. Historically, research in this area has taken two basic approaches to simulated intelligence: symbolic and empiric. The first approach uses first-order logic and symbolic processing. For example, expert systems simulate the knowledge of human experts using rule-based programs to gather information and make sequential decisions on the basis of facts and logical branching. These systems require human experts to construct the decision models necessary to simulate human information processing. Expert systems are used to standardize complex procedures and solve problems with clearly defined decision rules (Lawrence, 1993).

The empirical approach to machine intelligence has focused on the development of algorithms that adapt or self-modify in response to information. Artificial neural networks (also called associative memories, connectionist models) were originally developed as mathematical theories explaining the behavior of interconnected biological nerve cells found in animal life. The history of neural network theory leading up to modern neural network statistical methods is presented in the next chapter.

3

NEURAL NETWORK THEORY, HISTORY, AND CONCEPTS

As a class of statistics, neural network analysis is unusual in that many of its central concepts originated in fields other than statistics. The scientific history of neural network theory is rich with contributions from many different disciplines, including psychology. Although it is not necessary to know this history to use artificial neural networks (ANNs), this chapter introduces vocabulary and concepts that appear later in the book. Key concepts are italicized in the text and defined in the glossary at the end of the book.

EARLY THEORIES

In 1791, Italian scientist Luigi Galvani discovered that electrical activity stimulated muscular action in frog legs. Other important early work is described in the medical literature of the early 19th century. Cadaver studies had produced maps of the gross anatomic structures of neural tissue connecting the brain, spinal cord, and extremities, but theories regarding the function of these structures were still debated.

German physician Alexander Kolliker applied the newly invented microscope and carmine-staining technique to describe the interconnected microstructure of nerve cells (Kolliker, 1853). In the same period, Alexander

Bain, a Scottish psychologist and empirical philosopher, proposed his theory of psychophysical parallelism linking perception to mental and motor activity and describing what may be the first mathematically expressed theory of memory formation as a stimulus response (Bain, 1873).

Bain's (1873) research with perception and physiological response influenced British philosopher Herbert Spencer and American physician and psychologist William James. Both men published theories proposing that interconnected nerve cells were a medium of electrical activity. James (1890) proposed that nerve tissue was a conduit used by the body to "balance" electrical flow between the brain and the body. Specifically, James theorized the following:

1. Thoughts and bodily actions result from currents flowing from brain regions with excessive electrical charge to regions having a deficit of electrical charge.
2. Flow intensity is proportional to current flow rate, which in turn is proportional to the difference in charge between the two regions.
3. When these processes are simultaneous or in immediate succession, the recurrent flow in one neural pathway triggers a mutual excitatory response in the other.
4. Nerve currents pass most efficiently through pathways used most frequently.

Bear in mind that when the theories of James and Spencer were published, phrenology (the study of lumps on the skull as a guide to human ability and behavior) was considered respectable science. The prescient nature of these ideas found support over the next half century.

MODERN THEORIES OF NEURAL PROCESSES

In the 1930s, mathematical physicist Nicolas Rashevsky (1935) proposed the use of differential equations, energy minimization, and other concepts from physics to describe how nerve cells and neural network electrical flow might relate to motor activity, cognition, and perception. Working at the University of Chicago, Rashevsky brought together Warren McCulloch, a biologist, and Walter Pitts, a statistician. In 1943, McCulloch and Pitts published a mathematical theory of neural behavior that significantly influenced future research activity in digital computing, expert systems, and neural processing, as well as neurophysiology.

The McCulloch–Pitts neuron is a simplified model of a biological neuron diagrammed in Figure 3.1. According to this early theory, internal neuron activity is governed by five principles:

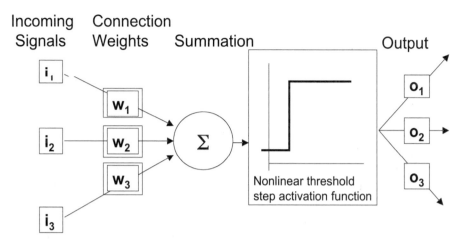

Figure 3.1. The McCulloch–Pitts binary neuron (McCulloch & Pitts, 1943).

1. Neural activity is binary (activation is either on or off).
2. Neurons have a fixed activation function so that any given input pattern always generates the same output.
3. Neuron activation is immediate; input stimulus results in output response with no delay except for that occurring in the synaptic junctions between neurons.
4. Any inhibitory input to the neuron will prevent it from turning on.
5. The connections between neurons do not change (Caudill, 1990).

Although flawed as a paradigm for biological neural activity and limited in terms of problem-solving ability, the McCulloch–Pitts neuron formed the basis of modern neural network theory by mathematically representing a model of neural activation that remains central to subsequent neural network designs. The McCulloch–Pitts neuron consisted of inputs, *connection weights* (a weighting scheme for connections between neurons), a summation function, and a hard limit or step *transfer function* that determined what value the neuron's output would take for a given set of inputs.

A vector of input values $(x_1 \ldots x_n)$ representing a series of data points from the outside world (or other neurons) is multiplied by a set of weights $(w_1 \ldots w_n)$ representing an excitatory or inhibitory connection between the input source and the receiving neuron. The weighted inputs are then summed. If the sum of the weighted inputs exceeds a certain threshold, the output equals one. If the threshold value is not met, the output is zero. This activation function can be expressed as follows:

$$\text{net}_i = \sum_{j=1,}^{n}(w_{ij}*o_j)$$

where net_i = neural output signal value for neuron i; W_{ij} = weight of the synaptic connection between neurons i and j; and O_j = the output of neuron j. The net output signal value for neuron i equals the sum of the weight times the input signal for all inputs to neuron i from neuron j starting at output of neuron $j = 1$ and ending at $j = n$ (Kosko, 1992).

McCulloch and Pitts (1943) demonstrated that these neurons can be used to compute Boolean logical operators and, when linked in networks, can solve more complex logical operations. The central problem of the McCulloch–Pitts neuron was that each set of weights for each neuron had to be calculated in advance to solve a particular problem. There was no procedure for adjusting the connection weights between neurons so that the network could self-adjust to solve different problems. In short, the McCulloch–Pitts neuron had no *learning rule*.

In 1949, psychologist Donald Hebb was seeking to explain how neurons are physically changed during learning. Hebb theorized that,

> when an axon of cell A is near enough to excite a cell B and repeatedly or persistently takes part in firing it, some growth process or metabolic change takes place in one or both cells such that A's efficiency, as one of the cells firing B, is increased. (Hebb, 1949, p. 62)

The idea that neural connections vary in strength according to how often a particular neural pathway is stimulated became known as Hebb's law. Hebbian learning was quickly integrated into mathematical models of neural behavior, most notably by Frank Rosenblatt, a biologist at Cornell University.

Building on the work of McCulloch, Pitts, and Hebb, Rosenblatt (1958) invented a model of the optic nerve of the common housefly. This early class of artificial neurons was collectively known as *perceptrons* and received a great deal of popular and research interest throughout the 1960s. Rosenblatt demonstrated that a network of these two-state (on–off) neurons, using a variation of Hebb's law, was capable of classifying input data (simple geometric shapes) and making threshold logic operations; he also showed that a self-adjusting system could retain information and self-modify as a result of training. Rosenblatt's refinement of McCulloch and Pitt's binary neuron is diagramed in Figure 3.2.

Rosenblatt's (1958) perceptron learning theorem held that a perceptron could learn anything it could represent. Representation refers to the ability of a neural network to simulate a function from sample data. Learning requires a systematic procedure for adjusting the network weights to produce that function. Rosenblatt's perceptron training algorithm operationalized

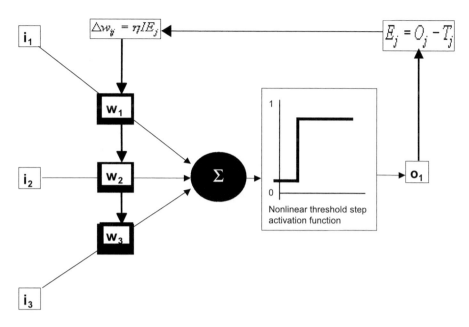

Figure 3.2. Rosenblatt's (1958) perceptron incorporating Hebbian learning.

Hebbian learning theory to challenge McCulloch and Pitts's (1943) fifth rule of neural behavior, which stated that connections between neurons are fixed. Rosenblatt's perceptron convergence theorem held that,

> Given an elementary alpha-perceptron, a stimulus world W, and any classification C(W) for which a solution exists; let all stimuli in W occur in any sequence, provided that each stimulus must reoccur in finite time; then beginning from an arbitrary initial state, an error correction procedure will always yield a solution to C(W) in finite time. (Rosenblatt, 1958, p. 390)

This method for training a network to find the correct input weights and threshold values is summarized in Figure 3.3. Using this supervised training procedure, the network will modify the input weights until the network will correctly classify a group of inputs in a finite number of iterations.

Two years after Rosenblatt published his work with perceptron networks, electrical engineers Bernard Widrow and Ted Hoff patented the adaptive linear element, or ADELINE (Widrow & Hoff, 1960). Designed as an analog noise reduction filter for digital signal processing, the ADELINE is a single neuron with a simple additive activation function, a linear transfer function, and one modifiable synapse for every element in the input pattern (see Figure 3.4). The ADELINE and the ADELINE network (multiple adaptive linear elements dubbed MADELINE) became one of the most

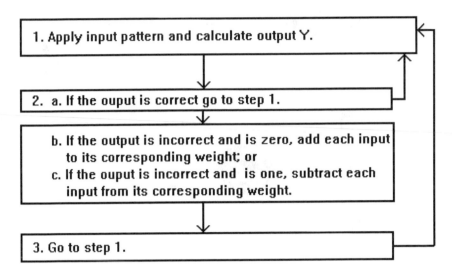

Figure 3.3. Summary of Rosenblatt's supervised training procedure for perceptron networks (Wasserman, 1989).

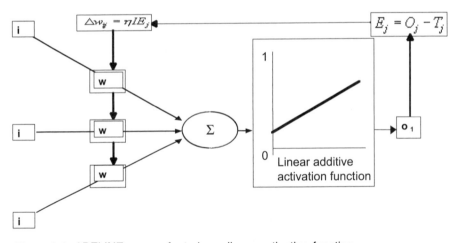

Figure 3.4. ADELINE neuron featuring a linear activation function.

commonly deployed neural network technologies. They are used in echo cancellation in long-distance telephone systems, real-time process control in medical and industrial applications, and computer modem technology, among many other current applications.

This was a significant development because with the ADELINE, Widrow and Hoff (1960) introduced a variation of the perceptron training algorithm able to process continuous inputs and outputs—the simple, but powerful, least mean square (LMS) or *delta rule*. The ADELINE uses the

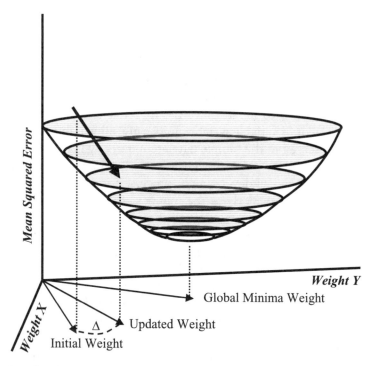

Mean Squared Error

Weight Y

Global Minima Weight

Updated Weight

Δ

Initial Weight

Weight X

Figure 3.5. Gradient descent of the connection weight matrix under the delta rule (Caudill & Butler, 1992).

LMS regression procedure to continuously modify the connection weight matrix to minimize the difference between the network output and the desired output (i.e., the observed actual value). The delta rule minimizes overall mean square error by multiplying the difference between the actual and desired output times the values of the inputs, times the learning rate:

$$\Delta w_{ij} = \eta(T_i(t) - a_i(t))o_j(t),$$

where Δw_{ij} is the change in the weight of the connection from neuron j to neuron i, T_i is the training input or correct answer, t is the specific time, a_i is the activation for neuron i, o_j is the output of neuron j, and η is the learning rate.

The delta rule is a *gradient descent algorithm* geometrically interpreted in Figure 3.5. When plotted in two dimensions (x,y), the mean square error versus the possible weight vectors show a parabola (a hyperparaboloid in N dimensions; Caudill, 1990). The total mean square error is a quadratic function of the weight vector. The delta rule modifies the weight vector to minimize its mean square error, iteratively moving the connection weight matrix down the negative gradient toward the bottom of the parabola to the ideal weight matrix, or point of LMS error. In this way, the delta rule modifies the connection weights between neurons until the objective function is fitted as closely as the data will allow.

This process is analogous to fitting a regression by adjusting beta weights to minimize square error, a fairly routine statistical exercise. Using a gradient descent learning rule to fit an objective function is quite different from manual adjustment of variable weightings because all variable combinations and surfaces observed in the sample data are iteratively mapped until incremental improvement stops. Although a human statistician could perform such an exhaustive model development process, it is unlikely to be time or resource efficient—particularly as the number of dimensions increase.

Because the delta rule requires the training term T_i, representing a known correct output (an independent variable) for each input (dependent variable), it cannot be applied to hidden-layer neurons for which the correct output value is unknown. Hence, the delta rule applied only to single-layer neural networks or the output layer of multilayered nets used to estimate the value of an independent variable. *Supervised networks* are ANNs trained to map sample inputs to matching outputs for estimation as explained later in this chapter.

In the mid-1960s, Massachusetts Institute of Technology (MIT) professors Marvin Minsky and Seymour Papert identified an entire class of relatively simple problems that cannot be solved by a single-layer perceptron network (Minsky & Papert, 1969). In their book, *Perceptrons*, Minsky and Papert demonstrated that the perceptron is limited to functions that are linearly separable, that is, problems in which sets of points (corresponding to input values) can be separated geometrically by a line, plane, or hyperplane. Restriction to linear separability limits a single-layer perceptron network to simple problems and severely limits utility with multivariate functions in which the underlying relationships are nonlinear.

As a result of these influential and somewhat disparaging findings, research interest and funding for ANN research languished for nearly a decade. Minsky remained at MIT and channeled his research interests into serial processing applications of machine intelligence. Some research on neural networks continued through the 1970s but at a reduced level (Klimasauskas, 1991; Lawrence, 1993).

Not all research activity came to a halt, however, and one important development during this lull was the first description of *self-organizing maps* (Willshaw & von der Malsburg, 1973). Self-organizing maps (SOMs) were put forward as a model of the topological structures in the brain that process sensory input. Neural receptor cells, each tuned to perceive signals in a specific range, occur in the brain as an array (in a grid pattern). As incoming signals of varying frequencies are processed, cells tuned to receive signals that occur more often are activated more frequently and self-organize into a place-coded frequency distribution or *topological map* of the incoming signal frequencies. The resulting pattern reduces the complexity of the incoming signal for use by higher order processors using comparatively simple connections.

Unlike perceptron networks that are trained to map inputs to known outputs, self-organizing neurons agglomerate sample cases on the basis of geometric proximity. SOMs can be described as a constrained form of *k*-means clustering in which cases in high-dimensional space are mapped to a two-dimensional surface called a topological map (Hastie, Tibshirani, & Friedman, 2001). Self-organizing neurons use *competitive learning* to reduce dimensionality while maintaining essential features of the data in a simpler form. An application of SOMs to reduce dimensionality and to cluster related cases in attitude survey data is described in chapter 8. In general, SOMs are used for exploratory analysis analogous to clustering and factor analytic procedures. Similarly, SOMs require informed interpretation of collapsed dimensionality and groupings of cases.

INNOVATION DRIVES RENEWED INTEREST

In the 1980s major contributions to neural network theory were made that led to a resurgence of interest in neural computation research. Three developments in particular are of interest to organizational researchers interested in using ANNs. Teuvo Kohonen's (1982) publication of the Kohonen self-organizing map improved the mathematics of earlier work and is the type of SOM described in this book. John Hopfield's (1982) introduction of energy surfaces to interpret network behaviors and the widely published series by Rumelhart, Hinton, and Williams (1986) on *backpropagation* networks have applications described in this book.

John Hopfield (1982) showed that information can be stored in a dynamically stable, symmetrical recurrent neural network. He also showed that neural network basins of attraction are analogous to spin glasses and energy surfaces in statistical mechanics. Spin glasses are quadratic differential equations describing the behavior of energy systems seeking equilibrium. The reason that Hopfield's simile is included here is that it introduced the use of surface response graphical analysis as a way of visualizing gradient descent, a technique that is quite useful for interpreting the processing of a trained neural network.

Neural networks compute geometric dimensionality. Each new example set of independent variables (an input vector) is positioned by the network in a dimensional space equal to the number of inputs. Each point in this hyperspace model defines a possible configuration of connection weights. As the network is trained, the connection weights between neurons are recursively adjusted for as long as the *error term* continues to decrease. At this point, it may be useful to refer again to Figure 3.5 in which the directional arrow pointing downward into the parabolic error surface shows the direction of gradient descent to the position of global minimum error, or *global minima*.

One way to visualize the "terrain" being mapped by the network is to draw a picture of the *computational energy surface*. The computational energy surface is used to represent the behavior of a neural model in three of *x* dimensions. Basins of attraction, global and *local minima*, convergence, and other features of the energy surface can be represented using surface response graphs available in statistical and neural network software. Graphic representation is useful for identifying nonlinearity and interpreting variable interactions in relation to both minimum error convergence and independent–dependent relations. Examples of surface response graphs and wire frame graphs used to interpret neural network mapping are explained in chapter 5. Examples of neural network interpretation using graphical analysis appear in chapters 7 and 8.

Other significant work by Ackley, Hinton, and Sejnowski (1985) and Rumelhart et al. (1986) showed that networks of fully connected perceptron processors using continuous, sigmoidal activation functions (explained later in the chapter) could solve nonlinearly separable representation problems. Minsky and Papert's (1969) proof that single-layer perceptron networks could not solve such problems did not apply to multilayer networks that used error backpropagation. Backpropagation of error settled the major concerns raised by Minsky and Papert.

BACKPROPAGATION NEURAL NETWORKS

The backpropagation training algorithm, also called the generalized delta rule, is a nonlinear extension of the LMS algorithm. Overcoming the limitations of the perceptron and ADELINE–MADELINE technology, backpropagation was hailed as a computationally efficient way to train multi-layered networks to represent nonlinearly separable pattern functions. Back-propagaton reawakened research interest in the capabilities and behavior of neural networks after the hiatus following the publication of *Perceptrons*.

The origin of backpropagation mathematics has been traced to the stochastic approximation learning theory literature of the 1950s (White, 1989a). Paul Werbos (1974) published the theorem as "dynamic feedback" in his Harvard University dissertation in political science and applied it in economic forecasting. Parker (1985) derived the same equations as "learning logic" in a product licensing report for MIT in 1985. Y. Le Cun (1985) is also commonly cited as a coinventor of backpropagation. Rumelhart et

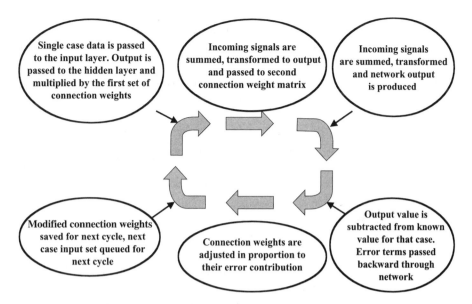

Figure 3.6. Training cycle of backpropagation networks.

al. (1986) popularized the generalized delta rule in the *Parallel Distributed Processing* volumes of the late 1980s and introduced a broad interdisciplinary audience to neural network capabilities and applications. The mathematics of backpropagation as given by Rumelhart are provided in the Appendix.

Backpropagation networks and their kin are used to estimate or classify values of an independent (output) variable. The term backpropagation refers to how the network is trained. Like the ADELINE and the perceptron learning procedures, the generalized delta rule also contains an error term used to teach the network if its output is correct or not. The training process consists of a forward pass of the data, in which the network processes a single input vector, updates the connection weights between neurons, and produces an output. A backward pass of the data beginning at the output layer follows. An error term, representing the difference between the actual and the desired output, is passed back (backpropagated) through the network as a partial derivative of the transfer function. A vector of transformed error values becomes the error term for the previous layer successively until the first layer is reached. Backpropagation of error is used to modify each connection weight in previous network layers in proportion to its relative contribution to error. In training, convergence occurs when the error term stabilizes or reaches a predefined threshold (Rumelhart et al., 1986). Back-propagation training is an iterative procedure involving six steps performed as each new case is presented and represented to the network. This is summarized in Figure 3.6.

The effect of backpropagation is to minimize the aggregate mean square error between the network's output and the known sampled independent variable. As such, backpropagation operates as a *stochastic approximation* algorithm in which the connection weight matrix converges at a solution of minimum error. For more information on backpropagation training, see Reed and Marks (1999).

These and other developments in the 1980s launched a resurgence of interest in neural network research that continues today. For the purposes of this book, we have covered the essential elements of neural network theory on which the applications in organizational research presented in this book are drawn. We acknowledge that the pace of research in the past decade has quickened and that more recent developments in neural network theory have not been described. The field has an active literature, including the refereed *Transactions on Neural Networks* of the IEEE (the Institute of Electrical and Electronics Engineers) and the International Neural Network Society's *Neural Networks*. There are dozens of other specialized journals and hundreds of online resources for the interested reader. The intellectual history of ANNs and artificial intelligence is the subject of many books, and the interested reader is encouraged to review Anderson and Rosenfeld (2000), Bailey (1996), and Crevier (1993).

A TAXONOMY OF MODERN ARTIFICIAL NEURAL NETWORKS

Networks of individual neurons can be configured in a variety of architectures. Some networks use only a single layer, whereas others use multiple layers. Input and output connections between neurons can flow forward or backward through the network. If a neuron's output is never dependent on the output of subsequent neurons, the network is of the feed-forward type in which incoming signals flow only in one direction. Other types of networks use feedback loops in which the output of some neurons is fed back as input to other neurons (Figure 3.7).

Neural networks are also classified by their training algorithm or learning rule. A *supervised network* (like the backpropagation networks) has its output compared with known correct values for each input set during training and uses the difference to adjust its weights accordingly. An *unsupervised network* is not provided with corrective supervision but instead learns to associate through trial and error. Special purpose simulators such as the bidirectional associative memory and Hopfield networks are constructed, not trained.

At a basic level, the type of neural network to use for a given modeling problem is determined by the purpose of the analysis and the available data. Neural net applications described in this book are limited to feed-forward,

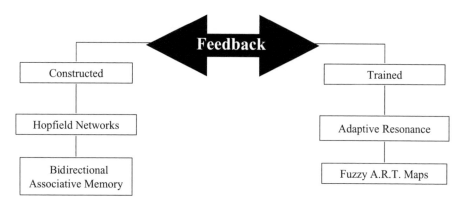

Figure 3.7. Feedback neural networks.

nonlinear neural networks (see Figure 3.8). Kohonen networks or SOMs are used to reveal natural clustering and association for exploratory and interpretive analysis. SOM networks are classified as *unsupervised* because they are trained to map internal structural elements and relations within a data set. Kohonen networks are used to group similar cases. As with factor and cluster analysis, rational interpretation of groupings challenges the investigator to understand the underlying processes and theoretical implica-

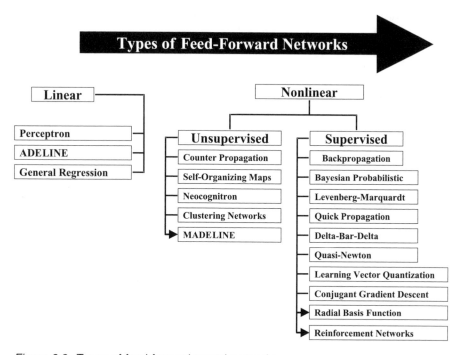

Figure 3.8. Types of feed-forward neural networks.

tions of the trained SOM. More on the theory and application of SOMs for the analysis of survey data appears in chapter 8.

SUPERVISED FEED-FORWARD NEURAL NETWORKS DESCRIBED IN THIS BOOK

Supervised feed-forward networks are trained to map the structural relationships between a set of independent variables and one or more dependent variable. When the objective of the analysis is to produce a predictive model for the estimation of a continuous, ordinal, or nominal output on the basis of a given set of inputs, supervised networks are used. Backpropagation and radial basis function networks are a group of supervised feed-forward neural nets that have been applied to a wide variety of modeling problems with good results. Behavioral prediction models described in chapter 5 are based on derivatives of backpropagation.

Backpropagation networks are of the supervised feed-forward type like that shown in Figure 3.9. Some neural network software packages (e.g., STATISTICA Neural Networks by StatSoft, Inc., 2003b; NeuralWare Predict by NeuralWare, Inc., 2004) have adopted an architectural reporting convention in which the number of neurons in each layer is listed in sequence separated by colons. For example, a network architecture consisting of a five-node input layer, a three-node hidden layer, and a two-node output layer would be described using 5:3:2 nomenclature.

A typical feed-forward network contains an input layer of neurons, one or more hidden layers, and an output layer. In most classification,

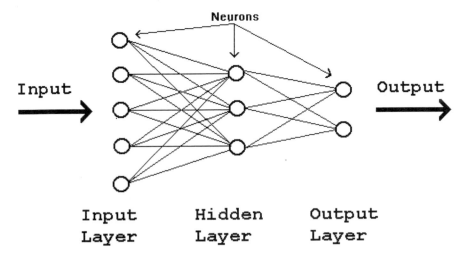

Figure 3.9. A fully connected feed-forward network with architecture 5:3:2.

optimization, and prediction applications, the number of input neurons corresponds to the number of input or independent variables. The number of output neurons corresponds to the number of criterion or dependent variables to be estimated by the network. For backpropagation, no quantitative criterion for the determination of the optimum number of hidden layers or neurons in each hidden layer has been generally recognized (Kosko, 1992). However, experienced neural network analysts have developed many heuristics or rules of thumb that guide neural network model development (Reed & Marks, 1999).

In practice, backpropagation networks rarely contain more than two hidden layers, with one being most common. Finding the right number of hidden layers and neurons involves a process of "tuning," in which various architectures and network parameters are varied systematically. Modifications proportional to changes in improved performance are retained; otherwise, adjustments are rejected and experimentation continues. This process goes on until no further performance improvements are obtained. Some neural network software programs feature network architecture optimization schemes involving the ranking and deletion of hidden neurons that contribute minimally to the objective function (NeuralWare Inc., 1994). In another approach, *cascade optimization*, one systematically adds hidden-layer processing elements (neurons) to the network until incremental performance gains cease (Fahlman, 1988). A more detailed set of heuristics for neural network development are described in detail in chapter 5 of this book.

Applied problem solving with neural networks, particularly for behavioral prediction, is increasing. One growing application is in the area of employee selection. The use of a backpropagation network to estimate a continuous dependent variable (predicted length of service) on the basis of a given set of independent variables is described in chapter 7. In that application, a neural network was trained to identify applicant characteristics associated with higher length of service. The output of the model was reported to hiring managers in the process of evaluating applicants and was used to inform employee selection decisions in a high-turnover hourly job with good results. Practical applications like this are valuable. However, neural network tools are perhaps more valuable for exploratory and confirmatory research to improve our understanding of human behavior in organizations. The next chapter discusses how to use neural networks in relation to theory building.

4

NEURAL NETWORKS AS A THEORY DEVELOPMENT TOOL

Although it has been argued that artificial neural networks (ANNs) have the potential to offer new insights into long-standing problems in organizational research, the basis of the argument lies in ANNs' ability to generate more robust empirical results compared with conventional multivariate statistical methods (see Collins & Clark, 1993). This logic is both compelling and seductive because organizational psychology research is focused on mapping relationships between predictor and outcome variables with practical consequences (e.g., job performance, employee turnover). Thus, it is not surprising that organizational psychologists are interested in ways to improve predictive accuracy, as it is a large part of what they do.

The more subtle and seductive part of this argument lies in its implicit link to the efficacy of the field itself. Research in organizational psychology and microelements of organizational behavior has been criticized as stagnant and repetitive (O'Reilly, 1991). Researchers, thus, have been faced with the prospect of explaining persistent, poor effect sizes relative to theory-driven expectations. It might be argued that these results are part of the scientific method and should be accepted in that context; that is, as an objective and replicable set of findings. However, when levels of explained variance are so consistently low that the value of the field is subject to question (or ridicule), it is natural to think that we might have overlooked something important.

An examination of the evolution of research in the field suggests that a case can be made that researchers have addressed this issue by broadening the conceptual frame of their studies. Thus, what was seen as missing were both the number of variables included in research and the number of hypothesized interactions among them leading to more comprehensive models of the areas under study.

These "comprehensive" models produced limited improvement over their less complex predecessors; that is, incremental variables have not resulted in incremental variance. Coupled with consistent disconfirmation of intuitive relationships (e.g., job satisfaction and job performance), a quick fix in the form of a new statistical technique such as neural networks has a seductive appeal. That is, ANNs have the potential to reverse a history of disappointing results and, in this process, provide a response to critics who suggest that research in organizational psychology is ineffectual. The innovative nature of neural networks also addresses concerns that organizational psychology research is moribund; a case can be made that something new and interesting is taking place.

As appealing as this argument might be in making a case for neural networks in organizational research, it is specious. As we explain in this chapter, if neural networks are to be of any use in organizational psychology and organizational behavior, their value will come as a theory development tool; that is, as a means of looking at long-standing problems in new ways. Our focus is on the ability of ANNs to model both linear and nonlinear relationships among variables as a means of gaining new insights into old problems. The use of ANNs, in turn, must be tied to problems that are well grounded in theory, and the results must be interpreted in terms of theory and prior research findings. The chapter also addresses the change in mindset that is needed to use neural networks as an analytical technique and to make sense of the output from an ANN.

LINEARITY, NEURAL NETWORKS, AND ORGANIZATIONAL RESEARCH

Perhaps the most pervasive and unexamined assumption in organizational research is that of *linearity*. Virtually all of our hypotheses are linear and derived from theories that are grounded in the metatheoretical assumption of linearity. Indeed, linear thinking and linear models are so embedded in our research, when we state that x is related to y, it is possible to delete the word *linearly* as a qualifier. Further, keeping the assumption of linearity at a metatheoretical level allows it to remain unexamined. As such, the poor effect sizes and low levels of explained variance typical of studies in organizational research have been attributed to virtually everything (e.g., measurement error, sampling error, misspecification of process, and low statistical power) except the possibility that (at least some) relationships among key variables are not linear in nature.

Questioning this pervasive assumption can open up new lines of thought and new ways of looking at old problems. To begin with, the primary criticisms of the field of organizational psychology shift from what is there to what is missing. That is, the "usual suspects" for explaining the slippage between expected and actual results are no longer viable. Rather, researchers must examine the fundamental nature of the processes that they are studying and come to some conclusion about whether the assumption of linearity is tenable.

A CASE FOR NONLINEARITY IN ORGANIZATIONAL RESEARCH

The widespread assumption of linearity in organizational research is not without its reasons. Operating from a linear perspective has several advantages, most notably parsimony. Indeed, the burden of proof for incorporating nonlinear thinking into organizational research lies with the critics of the current state of the field for precisely this reason (i.e., linear models are far more direct and simple than are their nonlinear counterparts). As such, a case has to be made that linearity oversimplifies processes and leaves us with an incomplete view of the phenomena under study.

Several scholars have raised this issue and called for a new direction in organizational research. For example, Bettis and Prahalad (1995) suggested that many phenomena within the domain of the organization sciences cannot be captured by linear models. Similarly, Starbuck and Mezias (1996) questioned the pervasive assumption of linearity in organizational research as well as the linear methods that stem from it. Somers (1999, 2001) made a similar case that much of what is studied in organizational psychology might not be linear and called for the use of new methods to study long-standing problems.

As such, there seems to be a case for nonlinear thinking in organizational research. In considering the role of neural networks in such an endeavor, it is important to understand what an overreliance on linear thinking means with respect to both theory and empirical studies. The first part of the argument concerns theory development and revolves around the proposition that linear thinking cannot adequately capture relationships among some key variables in our field. Specifically, concerns have been raised about the assumptions of proportionality and consistency; that is, the idea that relationships are consistent across the entire ranges of the variables being studied as defined by a slope and an intercept (Starbuck & Mezias, 1996).

It is important to emphasize that the rejection of proportional relationships among variables is a conceptual argument (West, 1980). At issue here is whether linear models are sufficient to understand important questions in organizational research. Put simply, if the assumption of linearity is rejected, it means that how we conceptualize problems needs to change. Therefore, the first step in the process of incorporating nonlinearity into organizational research begins with theory building.

A movement away from linear thinking requires movement away from linear methods as well. Thus, the second part of the argument is an emphasis on the need for new methodologies. It is noteworthy that there is some confusion here about how to proceed, even among researchers who advocate this view. Guion (1991) and Starbuck and Mezias (1996) offered curve fitting as an alternative methodology to linear methods, whereas Bettis and Prahalad (1995) pointed out that there are nonlinear equivalents to many of the linear methods currently used in organizational research. Other researchers have relied on more sophisticated techniques tied to advances in computer simulations to capture linear and nonlinear relationships among variables. For example, Hanisch, Hulin, and Seitz (1996) used a computer simulation to study the relationship between job tenure and turnover, and Somers (1999) used artificial neural networks to model voluntary turnover.

These studies are noteworthy because they were conducted to gain new insights into well-researched topic areas rather than to determine if new methods produce better results. As such, neural networks are central to this rethinking because they provide insights into the full range of relationships among variables (linear and nonlinear) in a manner that can often be more useful than curve fitting and that is more general than are study-specific computer simulations. Thus, to the extent that progress in exploring nonlinear relationships among variables in organizational research has been slow because of a limited methodological toolbox, ANNs can begin to address this problem.

NEURAL NETWORKS AS A THEORY DEVELOPMENT TOOL

Neural networks have the capacity to play a dual role in theory development in organizational research. One role is confirmatory and the other is exploratory. With regard to the former, ANNs can be used as a confirmatory technique to establish the efficacy of a theoretical model. The purpose of such a study is to test the assumption of linearity. That is, the hypothesis that relationships among the variables are linear is formally tested with the expectation that the assumption of linearity would be supported.

This represents an important departure from most organizational research because it directly tests the metatheoretical assumption of linearity.

Because ANNs test the full range of relationships among variables, support for the linear model serves to provide solid evidence that it is, indeed, the most accurate model of reality.

Such a finding drives theory development because it provides a basis for adding new variables to theoretical models in cases in which the overall predictive efficacy of the model is not consistent with theory-derived expectations. That is, it makes sense to look for additional variables and processes to understand the phenomena of interest and to refine existing theory accordingly, because the researcher can be reasonably certain that latent nonlinearity is not an issue.

A test of the full range of the relationships among variables also provides a context for evaluating the possible influence of methodological artifacts on the overall explanatory power of the theoretical model in question. More specifically, one can make a stronger case about the relative effect of methodological problems on the robustness of empirical findings because the broader issue of the nature of the relationships among variables has been explicitly tested. Similarly, one can interpret corrections from statistical techniques such as meta-analysis with a greater degree of certainty that the "corrected" levels of relationships among variables are plausible.

When used in a confirmatory manner, therefore, ANNs can drive theory development by providing empirical evidence about whether further refinement of an established linear model is appropriate. Support for the linear hypothesis suggests that continued refinement of existing theoretical models is in order perhaps with concomitant advances in the operationalization of key variables in the model.

While this type of research effort might be seen as moving incrementally along well-established paradigms, it is the most appropriate course of action. Indeed, it is the only course of action because radical reformulation of a model that is linear to include nonlinear components serves only to build error into the system.

Of course, it is possible that the linear hypothesis is disconfirmed. The first sign that this is likely to be the case is the observation of more robust results from the ANN compared with conventional multivariate statistics. In cases in which nonlinearity is present, the neural network should generate better predictive accuracy using test data with respect to conventional linear statistics.

The presence of nonlinear relationships among key variables in the model can be confirmed by examining wire-frame graphs representing response surfaces among variables at various points in training of an ANN. Recall from chapter 3 that a linear response surface is defined by a plane in space. Nonlinear surfaces represent significant deviations from a simple response surface and are often characterized by steep peaks and deep valleys (see StatSoft, Inc., 2002).

Empirical findings from an ANN suggesting that a linear model is untenable cast doubt on the hypotheses derived; it thereby challenges the researcher to look at the problem in new ways. It is noteworthy that even if linear statistics produce findings that are statistically significant with the level of explained variance characteristic of typical studies in organizational research, it is still possible that the model is misspecified.

The argument stated above is based on the assumption of several independent tests from different samples yielding corroborative results. At this point, researchers interested in the topic area under consideration are faced with the prospect of considering a different approach if progress is to be made. Given that the processes in the model as tested have not been supported empirically and a confirmatory test of the linear model implies a strong expectation that it would be upheld, the question as to how to proceed is critical.

It is at this point in the research process that neural networks become a very useful tool in theory development. The findings from the ANN can first be used to explore the issue of why a linear model was proposed in the first place. Was it by default, so that the question of the form of the relationships among variables in the model was never explicitly considered but rather was assumed? Or is there a compelling reason to believe that the processes embedded in the model are linear in nature?

Debate and discussion about these issues serve to drive the process of theory development because scholars are forced to look at established theories and patterns of empirical findings in new ways. Exploring the patterns of nonlinearity identified by the ANN is a good starting point in evaluating established theories. Indeed, the issue at hand is making sense of the patterns uncovered by the neural network. In so doing, it might prove helpful to look beyond the traditional domain area of organizational theory into related areas for insights into the process and problems at hand. For example, if nonlinearity was evident in a study of the relationship among organizational commitment, turnover, and absenteeism, it might prove useful to look at theory and research on withdrawal behavior in domain areas outside of work, such as marriage.

In any event, when used to test the assumption of linearity in a confirmatory way, neural networks are useful in theory development whether or not the linear model is supported. If the linear model is supported, researchers are provided with a clear direction for the continued refinement and development of existing theory. If the assumption of linearity proves to be untenable, ANNs are useful in opening up new lines of thought.

While there are topic areas in organizational research in which theory and empirical research have advanced to the point at which the assumption of linearity can be tested, there are other areas in which this is not the case. Empirical findings typically are contradictory, disappointing, or both.

In such a case, it makes little sense to test a suspect theoretical model in a formal way.

Researchers are sometimes perplexed about how to proceed under these circumstances. For example, in considering the relationship between job satisfaction and job performance (a classic example of empirical studies producing a pattern of weak supportive results, contradictory results, and nonsupportive results), Guion (1991) suggested curve fitting as a back-to-basics approach to mapping the relationship among these two variables.

It is in these situations that ANNs can be a valuable research tool. However, it is important to note that when used in an exploratory manner, neural networks are analogous to exploratory factor analysis. Specifically, in exploratory factor analysis, a researcher is seeking to understand the underlying dimensionality of a set of items with the intention of simplifying n-dimensional space (see Kim, 1978). When used in an exploratory manner, in turn, neural networks serve to uncover shape and structure of the underlying interdependencies among a set of variables. Although a researcher might have some hunches or suspicions about how the variables under study are related, these hunches cannot be considered formal hypotheses.

Much of the value of neural networks in theory development lies in their use as an exploratory tool. The extent to which that value can be realized lies with the researcher and not in the inherent properties of ANNs. For example, if a researcher mindlessly uses a supervised neural network to screen hundreds or even thousands of variables in relation to a criterion variable, then he or she has conducted a fishing expedition from the point of view of science and theory development. We recognize that there are applied problems in management practice in which this is appropriate.

The fishing expedition, however, does not lie in the statistical technique used but rather is embedded in the research design. That is, a similar argument applies if the researcher used the same design (hundreds of predictors and one criterion), but instead of an ANN as the screening tool, he or she used stepwise regression. While it is true that the neural network will almost certainly produce better results than will stepwise regression, a sophisticated fishing expedition is still a fishing expedition.

It is extremely important, therefore, for researchers to design exploratory studies using neural networks with some degree of care. The purpose of the study should not be to use ANNs as powerful devices to screen many variables. Rather, it should be to learn more about potential new patterns of relationships among variables that make sense both logically and in terms of prior empirical findings. In other words, the value of ANNs lies not in their ability to make a case for "comprehensive" models but rather in their ability to extract new information about relationships among variables under study.

The nature of the relationships uncovered, in turn, has the potential to lead to new ways of thinking about old problems. Recall that ANNs are pattern recognition algorithms that extract relationships among the variables included in the network. Some of the patterns might be meaningful by helping researchers recast processes in new, interesting, and nonobvious ways. That is, neural networks have the potential to quickly identify complex interactions among variables that might never be uncovered with conventional analyses. In attempting to understand these relationships, researchers in turn might be pointed to theory and research in areas that are closely related to organizational psychology but that have previously been overlooked.

It is important to note, however, that a robust pattern of results generated by an ANN might be uninterpretable. That is, while a neural network might produce better results (e.g., more accurate classification or better prediction), it does not guarantee that these results mean something. More to the point, conducting sensitivity analyses or examining three-dimensional wire-frame plots of relationships among variables might lead to the conclusion that the results do not make sense in that they are not easily explained or are of little heuristic value.

Researchers are likely to view this outcome as a dilemma because they are reluctant to discard or discount the stronger empirical results produced by the ANN. The first steps in diagnosing this situation lie with the neural network itself. Recall from chapter 3 that overtraining is a potentially serious problem for neural networks. When a researcher is faced with relationships among variables that do not make sense, it is imperative to ascertain that the network was not overtrained. The next step is to consider the representativeness of the sample. Because neural networks "learn" patterns in data, sampling error is likely to be magnified by an ANN because it is highly sensitive to sample-specific idiosyncratic relationships. In this case, results might well be uninterpretable because theory is not intended to explain oddities in subsamples.

When faced with results that do not appear to make sense, it is up to the researcher to decide what to do with them. We suggest that findings that are clearly anomalous be viewed with extreme caution. After all, there is a difference between thinking differently and not thinking at all.

USING ARTIFICIAL NEURAL NETWORKS AS AN EXPLORATORY TECHNIQUE TO MODEL THE JOB SATISFACTION–JOB PERFORMANCE RELATIONSHIP

It is helpful to illustrate how neural networks can be used in the theory development process with a specific example. Perhaps one of the most counterintuitive and vexing findings in organizational research is the consistent lack of a relationship between job satisfaction and job performance. Although job satisfaction is hypothesized to be positively related to job performance, empirical testing has produced a consistent pattern of nonsupportive results that spans nearly five decades. Indeed, meta-analysis indicates that the corrected correlation between job satisfaction and job performance is not statistically significant (Iaffaldano & Muchinsky, 1985).

Failure to produce a significant relationship between satisfaction and performance has not been for lack of effort. Perhaps because this is a relationship that ought to be significant with clear implications for theory and management practice, researchers have devoted a great deal of effort to empirical testing.

As might be expected, methodological concerns tied to both measurement and perceptual error have been proposed as reasons why it has been difficult to find a meaningful level of association between these two variables (Guion, 1991). While methodological issues cannot and should not be dismissed as a factor in the consistently low correlation between satisfaction and performance, it is also reasonable to look to other factors as well.

Guion (1991) took this view and suggested that one factor that has been overlooked in the large number of studies of the satisfaction–performance relationship is the form of the relationship itself. In so doing, he raised the possibility that the relationship might be nonlinear with poor empirical results stemming from repeated testing of a nonlinear relationship with linear methods.

ANNs are, of course, one way to address Guion's (1991) concerns, but even without the benefit of his insightful paper, a case can be made to use neural networks to model possible nonlinearities in the job satisfaction–job performance relationship. The argument rests with the theoretical proposition itself. That is, when researchers were faced with repeated disconfirmatory results, they did not suggest that the hypothesis be amended. Rather, they attempted to repair methodological problems in previous research studies with the expectation that future studies would produce stronger observed relationships between satisfaction and performance. These later waves of research led to additional calls for methodological refinements, when a growing body of empirical evidence clearly opened the door to consider alternative forms of the relationship.

The second part of the case rests with the results of empirical testing. Repeated testing of the satisfaction–performance hypothesis failed to establish a statistically significant relationship between these two variables but did produce a range of outliers in which relationships were found to be both positive and negative. Albeit small in number, these findings provide additional clues that perhaps a linear model is not the best way to view the relationship.

The nuances of exploring a nonlinear hypothesis are important. In this instance, nonlinearity is addressed as a possibility. Neural networks, in turn, are used in an exploratory manner; that is, to examine the full range of possible relationships among variables as opposed to confirming the (presumed) linear relationship.

Somers (2001) took this approach and used a supervised neural network to examine relationships between work attitudes, including job satisfaction and job performance. Results from a Bayesian neural network were compared with those from traditional ordinary least squares (OLS) regression and produced better results. The Bayesian neural network explained 23% of the variance in job performance using training data and 7% using test data compared with 3% of the variance from OLS regression.

Although these results are hardly remarkable, the ANN did perform twice as well as OLS regression using test data. The value of the neural network analysis, however, lies not in the increment in explained variance but rather in the mapping of the job satisfaction–job performance relationship.

Somers (2001) presented wire-frame graphs at the end of training that depict relationships among job satisfaction, job involvement, and job performance. Figure 4.1 indicates a strong presence of nonlinearity among work attitudes and job performance in areas of sensitivity in which strong relationships among job satisfaction, job involvement, and job performance fall within circumscribed ranges of these variables. These relationships can be described as highly channeled.

Our main objective is not to interpret these findings in detail but rather to demonstrate their usefulness in theory building. First, the targeted relationships suggest that the pattern of findings with respect to job satisfaction and job performance produced by linear statistics is not necessarily contradictory. Indeed, a pattern of results that is mostly nonsupportive but with a smattering of findings that indicate moderate to even strong relationships between job satisfaction and job performance is easily explained by the ANN.

Strong relationships are likely to be observed when the range of the job satisfaction variable for any given sample (e.g., study) falls into the "sweet spot" where sensitivity is high and the satisfaction–performance relationship is strong. Because these ranges are circumscribed, one would expect only a few studies to provide strong or moderate support for the general hypothesis that job satisfaction is related to job performance. Furthermore, it is likely the job satisfaction variable falling mostly into the high sensitivity area in any given study is a random event. A search for commonalties among studies in which job satisfaction and job performance are related, therefore, is not likely to yield meaningful patterns, leading to confusion and frustration (which is exactly what has occurred in research on this topic).

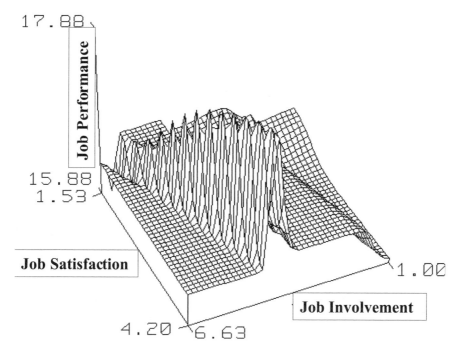

Figure 4.1. Wire-frame graph showing banded decrease in job performance as job satisfaction increases. From "Thinking Differently: Assessing Nonlinearities in the Relationship Between Work Attitudes and Job Performance Using a Bayesian Neural Network," by M. J. Somers, 2001, *Journal of Occupational and Organizational Psychology, 74,* p. 57. Copyright 2001 by the British Psychological Society. Reprinted with permission.

New insights can be also gained from the findings from the neural network research that have direct implications for theory building. At the most basic level, the results suggest that the job satisfaction–job performance hypothesis is bounded; that is, it is subject to much more restrictive boundary conditions than previously thought. Attempting to understand where these boundary conditions lie and why they are present, in turn, provides a basis for modification of the satisfaction–performance hypothesis.

Somers (2001) interpreted these findings to mean that job satisfaction and job performance are related only under optimal conditions, such as when roles are defined so that conflict is low or when people are highly involved in their jobs. Exploring these optimal conditions serves to redirect theory development efforts toward modifying the initial hypothesis to account for highly circumscribed relationships that appear to be tied to the socialization and integration of employees into organizations.

The overriding point here is that neural networks can be used to look at long-standing problems in organizational research in new ways even if the analysis begins from an exploratory perspective. It must be emphasized that placing too much weight on the results from any given analysis is to be avoided and, as is the case with conventional analyses, careful programmatic research is needed before modifications of existing theory can be justified. Nevertheless, there are many areas within organizational psychology and organizational behavior in which neural networks can be used to open up new avenues of research.

NEURAL NETWORKS AND COMPLEXITY THEORY

Complexity theory and the complexity sciences are gaining increasing levels of acceptance in the physical and biological sciences (Kaufman, 1993, 1995). Interest has been expressed in complexity theory in management research (McElroy, 2000) with the consensus view that complexity theory is gaining increasing acceptance in areas of interest to organizational psychologists (Hunt & Ropo, 2003; White, Marin, Brazeal, & Friedman, 1997).

As nonlinear dynamics are a key component of complexity theory (Axelrod, 1999), it might be argued that there is a natural or even compelling linkage between neural networks and the complexity sciences. At this point it is unclear if proponents of a "new science" based on complexity theory will also be seeking new methodologies. The debate is now focused on gaining acceptance of a new science view (Bird, Gunz, & Arthur, 2002). However, neural networks can be cast as a key methodological tool in the new science because of their ability to model nonlinear dynamics and self-organizing systems.

We view this extrapolation as having little or no merit. Recall from chapter 1 that neural networks are a set of pattern recognition algorithms with a long history of development that predates the rise of the complexity sciences (Swingler, 1996). Thus, ANNs were not designed specifically to test propositions from complexity theory, nor are they necessarily the best technique to do so. Further, and importantly, the use of neural networks in organizational research should not imply acceptance of or familiarity with complexity theory on the part of the researcher.

Our point here is that the use of ANNs does not imply an allegiance to a specific view of science. Researchers might use neural networks in an exploratory fashion to attempt to gain new insights into any topic area within organizational psychology. Such an application would not be an attempt to introduce concepts from the complexity sciences.

Neural networks are, however, amenable to introducing concepts from complexity theory into organization research, and they can be used for that purpose. For example, self-organizing maps can be viewed as an analog to the concept of self-organizing systems (see Mathews, White, & Long, 1999), and they certainly can be used to explore self-organization in organizational psychology. Neural networks, however, are best viewed as a tool. It is up to the researcher to determine what specific end they should be used for in any given study.

ARTIFICIAL NEURAL NETWORKS AS A FORCE FOR CHANGE IN ORGANIZATIONAL RESEARCH

A discussion of whether neural networks can serve as an engine of change in organizational research is a good way to bring to a close our discussion of the role of neural networks as a theory development tool. As we have seen in chapter 2, using neural networks requires scholars to think differently about the research process. But do they require researchers to think differently about the field itself? And if so, how differently?

Insights into how these questions might be answered can be found in looking at how the widespread adoption of new methodologies has affected theory development in organizational psychology. Perhaps the most significant methodological advance in organizational research in the last 20 years is the widespread acceptance of structural equation modeling (SEM). SEM has become so pervasive that LISREL, the primary statistical package used to conduct SEM analyses, was used as a verb, as in data being "LISRELed."

Widespread adoption of SEM required researchers to think more carefully about processes as ordered sequences of events because it was necessary to specify a weak causal ordering among variables to build structural equation models (Blalock, 1961). As a result, more attention was directed to how antecedent variables are linked to intervening variables in relation to a set of outcomes of interest. In so doing, almost all topic areas in organizational psychology and organizational behavior were studied more systematically because the issue of model fit (i.e., the overall plausibility of a set of hypothesized relationships) became as important as the amount of variance explained in the criterion.

The measurement approach required by SEM also required researchers to pay more attention to the psychometric qualities of perceptual measures. Confirmatory factor analyses provided better tools for establishing convergent and discriminant validity and determining the overall quality of any given measurement model.

All told, however, SEM is most accurately viewed as an incremental rather than a radical change in organizational research. Put simply, SEM with or without latent variables served to augment currently used methods and did not challenge conventional thinking.

Adoption of neural networks, on the other hand, represents a significant departure from the "typical" study in organizational psychology. Aside from a much steeper learning curve relative to SEM, researchers need to be prepared to understand and interpret findings that can deviate significantly from prior studies if nonlinearity is present in their data. Interpreting these nonlinear relationships, in turn, can require using theory from disciplines outside of the more circumscribed domain area under investigation (for a more detailed discussion of these issues, see chap. 9). As such, ANNs can be an engine that broadens our field by opening up new ways of looking at long-standing problems, but it must be remembered that the basis for innovative thinking ultimately will come from scholars and not from pattern recognition algorithms.

NEURAL NETWORKS AND APPLIED RESEARCH

Much of the resistance to the use of neural networks in organizational research seems to come from the general concern that ANNs will lead to a spate of atheoretical studies as researchers chase explained variance or some other measure of improved prediction in criterion variables of interest. These concerns are likely to be amplified by an examination of where and how ANNs have been used in applied settings. For example, neural networks are widely used to enhance credit-scoring models (Fensterstock, 2001), to detect financial fraud (Green & Choi, 1997), and to study the behavior of financial markets (Meissner & Kawano, 2001). In these applications, a neural network is trained against a behavioral criterion, and once it begins to break down relative to conventional statistics, the network is retrained so that new, more accurate weights are generated.

Applied problems in organizational psychology, however, have an underlying theoretical base, and researchers who ignore that base do so at their own peril. For example, neural networks are far more efficient in screening indicator variables for use in building selection models than are conventional multivariate statistics (Scarborough, 2002). However, one can make the same case for a credit scoring model built using a neural network. Where organizational psychology differs is that the final set of predictors for use in selection models, to extend our example, must be evaluated in terms of theory, prior research findings, and knowledge of the position(s) for which the selection model is being developed (this is not necessarily the case for a credit scoring model). Concepts such as job families become relevant for large-scale efforts so that one would expect to see commonalities among selection models for related jobs, and expected commonalities can be stated in advance (i.e., hypothesized) based on a clustering of jobs (which might be done with a self-organizing map).

Our point here is that a dustbowl empiric approach results from researchers and not from statistical techniques. The extent to which neural networks are used as black-box models in organizational psychology research will be determined by the extent to which researchers choose to apply them in this manner.

Neural networks have the potential to open up new avenues of research in organizational psychology and organizational behavior and to aid in the development of new, primarily nonlinear models. For this potential to be harnessed, researchers will need to think differently by looking at old problems in new ways. There is a learning curve associated with the mechanics of using ANNs, and with thinking differently, but we believe that it is well worth the effort.

5

USING NEURAL NETWORKS IN ORGANIZATIONAL RESEARCH

Most research problems in organizational research fall into one of three areas: prediction, classification, or clustering. As such, our hypotheses are usually centered on the relative contribution of predictor variables to a criterion or criteria, examining differences among groups, or assignment of variables or cases to distinct, meaningful clusters. Moving our discussion from the conceptual to the empirical, researchers in organizational psychology and organizational behavior have an extensive and established "analytical toolbox" to build the statistical models necessary to test their hypotheses. Readers should be familiar with these statistical methods, so there is no need for us to review them. Indeed, there are many excellent books on the topic of multivariate statistical methods.

Until recently, these techniques were the only tools that researchers had available, and as might be expected, they remain the predominant methods of hypothesis testing in organizational research. Advances in neural computing are slowly changing this state of affairs. It is important to note that the term *artificial neural network* (ANN) is generic and represents several neural computing paradigms (Swingler, 1996) which taken as a set can be used for classification, prediction, and clustering.

Recall from chapter 3 that ANNs are pattern recognition algorithms and, as such, do not correspond to the conventional statistics that most researchers in organizational psychology and organizational behavior use regularly. Thus, both academics and practitioners interested in using neural networks will find it necessary to think differently about how they approach data analysis and about the interpretation of findings. This chapter provides practical guidance for beginning to use neural networks.

GETTING STARTED: FACTORS TO CONSIDER IN EVALUATING NEURAL NETWORK SOFTWARE

As of early 2006, most of the larger providers of statistical software packages offer optional neural network development modules either as stand-alone application environments or as components in a general data mining analysis package. There are also a number of software companies selling neural network software for specific applications such as financial analysis, medical research, engineering applications, and survey research. In addition, there are many open-source neural network software packages available for almost every computing platform.

The following observations about what to look for in a neural network software program are offered as a starting point for the interested researcher. It is a good idea to consider the research and modeling projects that you will be working on, the type of data and data sources available, and the specific research questions and problems that you expect to work on using neural network analysis. With your specific research application in mind, the following considerations may prove helpful.

Ease of Mapping Relationships Among Variables

Research in most domain areas in organizational psychology and organizational behavior does not lend itself to nontheoretical or "black-box" models. That is, whether research using ANNs is conducted to address a specific issue in an organization or to advance academic theory, it is highly likely that the end-users of the research (be they scholars or managers) will want to know why the network performed as it did (especially if it outperformed conventional statistics).

This issue is a salient issue because in many applications areas in which ANNs are widely used, there is little concern for why the neural network has improved prediction. For example, in a credit-scoring application, a neural computing paradigm might be used for as long as it is effective and then retrained when it begins to underperform more conventional analyses. The end-user, in turn, is not very interested in understanding why the ANN offers superior results but rather is more concerned with the overall accuracy of the predictions resulting from the "black box." Because this is a large segment of the market for ANN software, many vendors concentrate on engineering software that optimizes adjustment of weights with less concern about what these weights might mean in understanding social–psychological processes.

Graphical mapping of relationships among variables is the best technique for gaining insights into how the network is making decisions and, thus, what it means for management theory and practice. Some software packages have advanced graphical functions built into them, such as SPSS's Neural Connection, which has now been integrated into their Clementine data-mining package. Others such as MATLAB's Neural Network Toolbox export data that can be used by MATLAB's extensive graphical capabilities (which requires learning MATLAB's graphics modules). Although allowing for data exports, many neural network packages do not have built-in or add-on graphical capabilities, requiring users to either purchase a high-end graphics package or use the barely adequate graphics of spreadsheet applications such as Excel.

We place a high weight on mapping relationships among variables and suggest that this be an important consideration in selecting neural network software. A demonstration version of neural network software will prove very helpful in assessing its graphics capabilities.

Visualization Tools for Training

Training an ANN is an involved and active process unlike conventional statistical analyses in which parameters are set (usually by selecting menu items in the statistical analysis software) to determine how the analysis will be structured. Given today's high-speed personal computers, results from conventional analyses are virtually instantaneous, thereby allowing the researcher to turn his or her attention to the findings. In some cases, post hoc analyses might be conducted, but they are after the fact and not part of the initial analysis.

Neural networks operate in an entirely different fashion. As emphasized throughout this book, researchers must actively *train* the ANN to *learn* patterns in the data and, in the process, reach a determination about when training is complete. There are no set rules to invoke that signify the end of training, nor is there a guarantee that two people training the same ANN will terminate training at the same point.

To make informed and intelligent decisions about training ANNs, it is important to have access to visual tools that capture and display the state of the network over time and at any given time. For example, if we use overall error (e.g., root mean square error [RMSE]) as a general indicator of network accuracy, it is helpful to have a visual tool that shows the rate of decline in RMS error over training cycles to help the researcher determine the rate at which the ANN is capturing patterns in the data. A very rapid decline in RMSE error at the start of training followed by more gradual declines over time is a desirable pattern that suggests that the initial starting parameters for training were set correctly. As declines in error begin to flatten out and become imperceptible over additional training cycles, this is a sign that learning is nearly complete and the researcher should become concerned about overtraining.

There are other parameters in training that are also well suited to visualization tools. RMS error is just one example. Different software packages handle visualization in different ways, and researchers have their preferences as well. We strongly urge that researchers evaluate the visualization tools with great care both within and between neural network software packages before making a decision about purchasing a specific ANN software package.

Neural Network Paradigms Included With the Software

At this point the reader should be well aware that there is no such entity as an omnibus neural network; rather, there are several distinct neural computing paradigms with varying characteristics and applications. Generally, ANN software includes more than one neural computing paradigm, and indeed, several packages are quite comprehensive (e.g., STATISTICA Neural Networks, MATLAB). Others are highly specialized, such as SOMine, which is restricted to self-organizing maps (SOMs).

It is highly unlikely that research in organizational psychology will require the full array of neural computing paradigms. Indeed, most topic areas can be addressed with a backpropagation neural network such as a multilayered perceptron and a SOM application. Most packages include an extensive array of backpropagation networks for use in prediction and classification, as well as a SOM tool. Other things being equal, the SOM application tends to be underfeatured compared with the other neural computing paradigms. We suggest that researchers who are heavily involved in clustering problems ensure that the SOM tool in a generic neural network package meets their needs.

Finally, it is important to note that there are many neural computing paradigms that are well suited to engineering applications, such as process control and signal detection, but are not suited for use in organizational psychology or organizational behavior (e.g., Boltzmann machines). We suggest careful investigation of the neural computing paradigms included in a software package to ensure that there is adequate representation of neural networks relevant to organizational psychology.

Preprocessing Capabilities

Effective preprocessing of input data is essential for the proper training of an ANN. Whereas virtually all documentation included in ANN application software discusses the importance of preprocessing especially with regard to handling outliers, many programs do not include preprocessing capabilities. Put simply, researchers must evaluate input variables including needed transformation of variable(s) and the entire input space with other statistical packages, and the transformed data must then be reentered into the ANN software package.

Other neural network packages provide extensive preprocessing capabilities, including visualization tools for the data before and after preprocessing. This integrated approach is very convenient, and we believe it is an important advantage to have in an ANN package. Finally, some software companies offer separate preprocessing software that is fully integrated with the ANN package but at additional expense.

Preprocessing is an essential step in using neural networks that cannot be bypassed. When choosing neural network software, one must map out how preprocessing is to be accomplished. Where and how preprocessing of data is done is not as important as having this capability somewhere in the researcher's toolbox. Our only caution is that the price of neural network software is not necessarily an indication that preprocessing tools are included in the package; that is, there are comparatively expensive packages that do not include preprocessing tools and relatively modestly priced packages that do include them.

Integration With Statistical Software Packages

Neural network software takes one of two forms. Most programs are stand-alone packages that are not designed as extensions of more conventional statistical software. Data are usually input and output as comma delimited, text delimited, or Excel spreadsheets. Thus, if one wishes to perform standard statistical tests on input or output data or use a standard statistical package such as SPSS or SAS to process input data (e.g., missing values, recoding), some degree of inconvenience will be experienced with stand-alone ANN software. Although the required file manipulation does not require a high level of technical skill, it can be time consuming especially with large data sets.

In contrast, comparatively fewer statistical software packages offer ANN modules of programs that are part of a family of analysis tools. Integration with the neural network package is much tighter as it is possible to move data throughout the program family with little difficulty (e.g., STATISTICA, MATLAB, SAS, SPSS).

For some researchers, the added convenience of a family of analysis tools is likely to be very important. When evaluating demo versions of ANN software, we suggest using personal data sets to get an idea of how the program handles data input and output rather than tutorial data supplied by the vendor (as it is already in the correct format).

Documentation

Most vendors provide extensive documentation with their ANN software packages. Documentation typically includes instructions for using the software program and a discussion of neural computing paradigms. That said, documentation varies in quality with respect to the latter topic. In some cases, brief descriptions of neural computing theory are offered, whereas in other cases extensive, high-level discussions of the theory and use of neural networks are offered.

The best documentation explains the logic and development of each neural computing paradigm included in the software. It then ties diagnostics and other indicators of effective training to the tools in the software program to guide the researcher in realizing the power of ANNs. Some vendors do an exceptional job in this area, whereas others are not as thorough.

Computing Platforms

Neural network software no longer requires the computing power of a high-end workstation. Virtually all software will run without problems on relatively modest machines. A 1-GHz Pentium is more than adequate to run most neural network software, and many programs are downward compatible to 233-MHz Pentium II machines. For Macintosh users, a G3 processor running at 400 MHz or higher is adequate to run most neural network software. Of course, training will take longer on a slower processor, but the more limited computing power will not affect the results from the ANN, only the time it takes to produce them.

Neural network software is available for the Windows, Macintosh, and UNIX operating systems. Windows offers the widest selection of neural network software packages, and most vendors offer Windows versions of their products. There is also a good selection of neural network software for UNIX operating systems, including Linux. As a general rule, UNIX packages tend to be geared more toward scientific and engineering applications, but there are ANN software applications that are well suited to problems in organizational psychology that run on UNIX.

With respect to Macintosh users, it is unlikely that ANN software will continue to be developed for the legacy OS 9 operating system or that current software will be maintained. The latest version of the Mac OS, OS X, is based on BSD UNIX. Several vendors have ported UNIX-based neural network applications to OS X using XWINDOWS (which is included in OS X 10.3). This trend is likely to continue, thus giving Macintosh users more access to neural network software. It should be made clear, however, that the XWINDOWS environment differs considerably from the OS X environment, and many functions within OS X are not available in XWINDOWS.

GETTING STARTED: CHOOSING THE RIGHT NEURAL NETWORK

The first issue to consider in using neural networks is making a decision about the appropriate neural computing paradigm. Some of the newer software packages offer artificial intelligence tools or "wizards" that ask a series of questions and then select a neural network for the research issue at hand (e.g., StatSoft, Inc., 2002). We strongly recommend against using wizards blindly to choose neural network paradigms. Rather, it is important that researchers make informed decisions on the basis of a thorough understanding of the properties and pitfalls of the neural network that they select.

The most basic choice is between supervised and unsupervised neural networks. Recall from chapter 3 that supervised networks (those trained with correct answers) require a data set that includes an outcome or a criterion variable and a set of antecedent or predictor variables. These neural networks "learn" patterns in the data by mapping relationships between the predictors and the criterion variables, and as such, supervised networks are appropriate to prediction and classification problems. Analogs among conventional statistical methods include ordinary least squares (OLS) regression, moderated regression, structural equation modeling, discriminant analysis, and logistic regression. In contrast, unsupervised neural networks group like items into clusters on the basis of similarities within a set of variables. Consequently, unsupervised networks are best suited to clustering and data reduction problems. Analogs include multidimensional scaling, k-means, and hierarchical cluster analysis.

We begin with a discussion of the most widely used unsupervised neural network, self-organizing maps, and then move on to the most common supervised network paradigm, feed-forward networks with backpropagation of error.

UNSUPERVISED NEURAL NETWORKS: USING SELF-ORGANIZING MAPS

Self-organizing maps (SOMs) are gaining popularity in areas such as finance and marketing (see Deboeck & Kohonen, 1998) but are not widely used in organizational psychology or organizational behavior research. They are sometimes referred to as Kohonen networks in deference to Teuvo Kohonen, who built the algorithm on which SOMs are based (see Kohonen, 1995). SOMs "learn" similarities among cases in a profile. Cases are then mapped such that similar cases are assigned to the same neuron, which serves as a placeholder in x-dimensional space. As data are passed through the pattern recognition algorithm many times, neurons with similar profiles are positioned next to similar points in space, leaving a surface that reflects patterns of similarities and differences of the variables in the original data set.

The primary differences between SOMs and conventional clustering techniques are that (a) data are passed through the neural network many times and (b) cases are assigned to "neurons" that migrate in n- (usually two-) dimensional space as case membership changes over the course of the analysis. Because the distances between neurons are meaningful, SOMs produce results that can be viewed as a cross between cluster analysis and multidimensional scaling.

A step-by-step guide to using SOMs as a clustering tool follows. We strongly recommend that researchers use this as a general guide and not as a substitute for gaining a thorough knowledge of the properties of SOMs.

Issue 1: The Dimensionality of the Map

Although almost all analyses using SOMs are based on two-dimensional space (Deboeck & Kohonen, 1998), SOMs are not inherently limited to a two-dimensional response surface. Most researchers choose two-dimensional maps because of their interpretability. Furthermore, because SOMs are inherently data reduction techniques, a meaningful two-dimensional solution is much more likely to serve most researchers' purposes.

Issue 2: The Size of the Map

One way of thinking about the architecture of a SOM once its dimensionality has been established is in terms of the number of neurons that define it. Taking a two-dimensional response space as an example, a 7×7 map (seven rows and columns) is comprised of 49 neurons (cf. Eudaptics, 2001; StatSoft, Inc., 2002).

It is necessary to build a map with an appropriate number of neurons. A map that is too sparse will not be sensitive enough to extract meaningful clusters in the data set. Conversely, a map that is too dense might lead to artificial splits within clusters or groups that have little practical or theoretical significance.

The number of variables in the analysis and interdependencies among them are critical to determining the number of neurons to be included in the map. For example, a rich data set that includes demographic, behavioral, and attitudinal variables will likely require a more complex map with more neurons than will a SOM that clusters product preferences on the basis of a limited number of questions about usage and attitudes.

When in doubt, we suggest that researchers err on the side of caution and include more neurons rather than less. A solution in which large pieces of the map are empty (no cases assigned to the neuron) is a clear indication that the map can be reduced in size with little or no loss of information.

Issue 3: Preprocessing

All neural computing paradigms are sensitive to outliers, and SOMs are no exception. Thus, input data must be examined (using histograms or scatter plots) for outliers. Either the outliers can be discarded or the data can be transformed to bring the distribution of a given variable into a better form.

If outliers are left in the data, it is very likely that the final map will be distorted as the fitting algorithm attempts to adjust the output space to accommodate outliers. For this reason, we emphasize that preprocessing of all variables is a critical part of using SOMs, and we urge researchers to pay careful attention to the distribution of each variable in the analysis.

Issue 4: The Number of Training Cycles

Data are passed through neural networks thousands or tens of thousands of times as the network adjusts weights to generate a solution. The researcher, as part of training, must determine how many passes of data are needed for the SOM to identify patterns of association among cases that allow them to be assigned to neurons on the map (Kohonen, 1995).

There is an element of subjectivity in determining when training should be terminated. Building skill in this area comes from experience and experimentation and develops over time. Overtraining (too many training cycles) results in patterns unique to a data set that are not generalizable. Conversely, an inadequate number of training cycles will lead to crude solutions that do not capture underlying interdependencies in the data set.

Diagnostics are used to evaluate the quality of a solution produced by a SOM (see Issues 5 and 6) and can be used to gain insights into the effectiveness of training. For example, high quantization error is indicative of undertraining because the reduced space does not map well to the original input variables. Overtraining is assessed more qualitatively. One indicator is the presence of small, fringe clusters that have little practical or theoretical meaning (much like "fringe factors" in factor analysis). For example, if a SOM produced a small cluster in which mean job satisfaction, intention to remain, and job search behavior were significantly higher relative to other clusters and the turnover rate for this cluster was zero or very low, the researcher should consider the possibility that the network was overtrained. That finding clearly makes no sense, runs counter to results from hundreds of studies, and is not easily explained. This suggests that it is an anomaly in the data that might have been captured by overtraining the network.

Issue 5: Determining the Number of Clusters

The outcome of a SOM analysis is a map of neurons organized by relative similarity. That is, neurons with cases that have similar characteristics will be in closer proximity on the map. The next task is to group these neurons into meaningful entities or clusters. Software packages such as Eudaptics SOMine provide a tool that estimates the number of clusters, thereby allowing an end-user to compare several different solutions. In other cases, it is necessary to compute summary statistics for each neuron on the map and determine areas of breaks and transitions.

This is a subjective decision that is similar to determining the number of factors in exploratory factor analysis (see Kim, 1978). It is handled in much the same way in that clusters are assessed on the basis of their value to the researcher (on the basis of theory or practice) and, after careful thought, clusters are either aggregated or retained.

Issue 6: Quantization Error and the Quality of the Solution

Because a SOM is a data reduction technique, the reduced dimensionality will not mirror the input data exactly. There will be some loss of detail when reproducing relationships among the original variables with the reduced dimensional space (Eudaptics, 2001).

Quantization error (QE) is a measure of the Euclidean distance between a specific case vector and the mapping of that vector's location assigned by the SOM. Like root mean square error (RMSE) used in backpropagation to measure distance between vector location and the dependent variable (the actual value that the network is estimating), it is an error term. Unlike RMSE, QE is the distance between the vector position and the collective position of other similar case vectors. Once training is completed, vectors of input variables are compared with their closest fit on the map, with differences termed as QE (Eudaptics, 2001). A good solution will have low QE across each neuron, which, in turn, sums to a low overall QE for the map.

Issue 7: Qualitative Assessment of the Quality of the Solution

Once the analysis is completed and clusters are defined, it is important to interpret the resultant profiles in terms of theory and practical considerations. The clusters ought to represent meaningful groupings that are useful in advancing theory or providing new insights into practical problems (see Deboeck & Kohonen, 1998).

In this regard, it is important that the solution produced by the SOM is useful. Low QE does not ensure usability or efficacy, so it is important that SOMs are evaluated both qualitatively and quantitatively.

SUPERVISED NETWORKS: TRAINING NEURAL NETWORKS FOR PREDICTION AND CLASSIFICATION

Recall that supervised neural networks are trained to estimate an independent variable from a set of dependent variables resulting in a model that can be used to estimate unknown values of the independent using observed inputs (dependents). As with regression or discriminant analysis, data requirements for model development include observed values of the independent variable (output) with matching values of the dependent variables (inputs) for each sample case. Experienced analysts will note that issues related to supervised training of a neural network are similar in some ways to model development using conventional procedures.

Issue 1: Selecting a Neural Computing Paradigm

A feed-forward neural network using the family of backpropagation algorithms will serve the needs of most researchers for both prediction (continuous criterion) and classification (categorical criterion) problems. These networks are often referred to as multilayer perceptrons, or MLPs (Swingler, 1996). It should be noted, however, that other neural computing paradigms can be used to solve prediction and classification problems. This issue is discussed under the section on learning rules.

In addition to the generic MLP, radial basis functions (Ripley, 1996) are also well suited to prediction and classification. Learning vector quantization networks have been shown to be effective in classification problems (Somers, 1999). We suggest that an MLP be used as a baseline and other neural computing paradigms be evaluated in terms of the results produced by MLPs.

Issue 2: Defining the Network Architecture

Once a neural computing paradigm is selected, it is necessary to build a network architecture. Neural network architecture refers to the number of processing elements or neurons in the input, hidden, and output layers of the neural network (Wasserman, 1989). The number of independent variables or predictors in the sample data determines the number of neurons needed for the first layer of the network. Continuous input variables require only one input neuron. Nominal variables with more than two categories require one neuron for each category. Most neural net software programs will create a one-of-N encoding for categorical variables automatically. Similarly, the number of output layer neurons equals the number of dependent variables or output criteria that the network is being trained to estimate or classify. The neuron count of the hidden layer or layers, however, is left to the discretion of the researcher and requires some discussion.

Backpropagation networks can be constructed with more than one hidden layer; however, research with multiple hidden layers indicates that most of the time more than one hidden layer is of little value in improving network performance (Ripley, 1996). Although there is no agreed-on procedure to determine the number of neurons in the hidden layer, it is useful to reinforce the point that mapping of the input to output variables occurs in the hidden layer. Therefore, the number of neurons has to be sufficiently dense to capture relationships among input variables with respect to a known outcome. As such, it is unlikely that a hidden layer with two neurons is sufficient to model relationships among a network with 10 input variables.

Identification of the optimum number of hidden units is essentially a trial-and-error process. Klimasauskas (1991) described a heuristic for determining the upper limit for the number of hidden units. This rule of thumb holds that there should be at least five training examples for every connection in the network. The trial-and-error process of optimizing the number of hidden units can be either destructive or constructive.

The destructive approach begins with a large number of hidden units. Each hidden unit is systematically disabled, followed by network testing. If performance improves, the neuron is disabled. The process is repeated for each hidden neuron until performance declines, the last disabled neuron is reinstated, and that number of hidden units is used.

The constructive approach starts with no hidden neurons, adding one at a time while testing for performance improvement until the addition of one more unit causes performance decline. A variation of constructive hidden unit optimization is based on the cascade-correlation paradigm invented by Fahlman and Lebiere (see Fahlman, 1988). This procedure begins network training with no hidden units. Input neurons are connected directly to the output layer. Hidden units are added one a time, with each additional

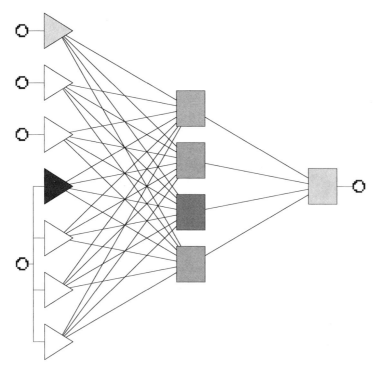

Figure 5.1. Neural network diagram with architecture 7:4:1 consisting of three continuous and one nominal input variable with four possible values, four hidden layer neurons, and one output neuron. Diagram produced with STATISTICA Neural Networks Version 6.0. Copyright 2002 by StatSoft, Inc. Printed with permission.

unit assigned to predict the current remaining output error in the network. Each hidden unit receives input from all previous hidden units and the input layer. Additional units are added until no further improvement is obtained.

Caudill (1991) and Klimasauskas (1991) made specific recommendations regarding hidden layers and hidden neurons. Both agreed that most neural applications can be solved by networks with three layers: an input layer, a hidden layer, and an output layer. Error terms backpropagated from the output layer decrease by one order of magnitude at each layer, rendering backpropagated error values almost meaningless when sent back more than two layers. Training time also increases dramatically with the addition of more layers and more hidden units. Finally, generalization (the ability of the network to recognize and apply learned pattern information to new input data) is enhanced by using the smallest possible number of hidden neurons.

Network architecture is often summarized using the convention described in chapter 2, in which the number of neurons in each layer is followed by a colon until all layers have been specified, as shown in Figure 5.1.

Careful thought about the complexity of the problem under study coupled with sensitivity to the size of the input vector that is to be passed through the network should allow an educated guess about the density of the hidden layer. Experimentation to help refine the initial network architecture is both appropriate and useful.

Issue 3: Data Preprocessing

To use neural networks effectively, one must review and, if necessary, preprocess the data set involved in the analysis. At the very minimum, variables should be standardized. Most neural network software does this automatically, but it is important to ensure that standardization has occurred. In addition, it is imperative that the data set be carefully examined for outliers. Outliers have the potential to greatly distort the training process and the solution provided by the neural network. When faced with outliers, researchers can delete the problematic variables or cases within a variable or they can transform the variable to reduce skewness or kurtosis.

A trained neural network will fit the frequency distribution of the sample data. When a neural network application involves pattern recognition among classes that differ in frequency, classification by the network will assign cases to the most commonly occurring categories to maximize accuracy (minimize error). Creating a training file with an artificial distribution in which all classes are equally probable can often improve the utility of the model (Klimasauskas, 1991).

Scarborough (1995) described training neural models to classify sales personnel by productivity using psychometric data. The most productive sales agents in the sample represented the top 15% of a normal distribution and the targeted subgroup for a hiring recommendation model. Networks trained with unadjusted sample data simply rejected all subjects to achieve 85% correct classification accuracy! Networks trained with a preprocessed training sample in which all levels of sales productivity were equally likely classified 77% to 84% of the sample correctly while allowing some candidates to "pass" the more stringent hiring recommendation standard. Thus, training the network with an artificial distribution forced greater complexity on the network, in effect making it work harder to identify the less commonly occurring cases.

The importance of data preprocessing cannot be overstated. A neural model can potentially simulate all functional relationships represented in training sample data. This "memorization" of the training sample includes modeling spurious noise and interaction effects that may be sample specific, leading to poor generalization. Alternatively, the presence of extreme outliers can slow convergence, as connection weight resources are allocated to accommodate rare cases. If sample size allows uncompromised statistical

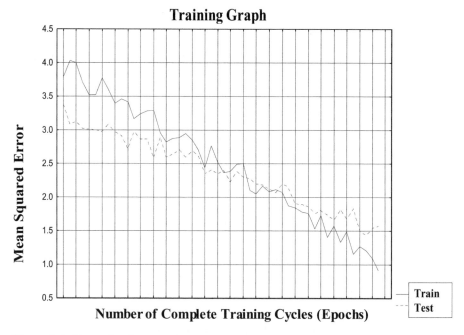

Figure 5.2. Example of a neural network training graph showing network root mean square error by training cycle on training and test sample data. Diagram generated using STATISTICA Neural Networks Version 6.0. Copyright 2002 by StatSoft, Inc. Printed with permission.

power, general model accuracy can be improved by removing problematic case records selectively from the training data.

Issue 4: Training

Once a neural computing paradigm and concomitant architecture have been chosen and data have been preprocessed, it is appropriate to train the network. Most software programs present a line plot of training progress as shown in Figure 5.2. We strongly urge researchers to become familiar with each training parameter so that they understand what it means and how it controls pattern recognition. It is appropriate to accept default values provided by software packages provided that the researcher is aware of how these values govern training. A discussion of each major training parameter for a feed-forward network follows.

Number of Training Epochs

The number of training cycles or epochs is the number of times that the network is exposed to every record in the sample data. A complete pass of all records equals one training epoch. The number of epochs necessary for training can vary widely depending on the size of the data set and the complexity of the data. If few cases are available, more epochs may be needed for the network to converge. Larger (more representative) data sets will require fewer training cycles if the data structures are fairly simple. In general, epochs of training increase with greater complexity.

As the network is trained, measures of network performance should improve. In Figure 5.2, root mean square error (RMSE) declines as training continues. The two lines represent RMSE of the network's output on two disjoint subsets of the sample data. The training set is the subset of data actually used during training to update the connection weight matrix. RMSE of the network output on a disjoint independent subsample (the test set) is used to determine if network learning is generalizing to new data. As a rule, when these two lines converge, it is a good time for training to stop. If the training performance continues to improve but the test performance remains stable, the network is overtraining (memorizing the training data).

The procedure for optimizing epoch size begins by selecting an initial epoch size, training the network for some preestablished number of cycles, testing the network, and recording network performance. By repeating this process incrementally and decrementally, the plotted accuracy measure will peak when the optimal epoch size has been tested.

Learning Rules and Parameters

Recall that the learning rule is the gradient descent algorithm used by a neural network to iteratively modify the connection weights in the direction of minimum error. Backpropagation software packages allow the user to specify the type of learning rule to be used by an entire network or by one or more layers of the network, or specify learning parameters at the level of individual neurons. Several learning rules that are common in many ANN software programs are discussed briefly.

The delta rule is the original backpropagation learning rule described in chapter 3. The cumulative delta rule is identical to the delta rule except that instead of changing weights with every pass of the data, the cum-delta rule accumulates weight changes over several passes of the data before modifying the connection weight matrix. This accumulation allows for a quicker descent toward the minimum solution, which improves training time and may allow gradient descent to be less susceptible to local minima.

A third learning rule option is called the normalized cumulative delta rule. The norm-cum-delta option retains the advantage of accumulated error weight updates but allows for greater flexibility in optimizing the epoch size (discussed subsequently) while training the network. Unlike the cum-delta learning rule, the norm-cum-delta rule divides the learning coefficient by the square root of the epoch size, which eliminates the need to adjust each learning coefficient each time the epoch size is altered.

Other training algorithms or neural network paradigms that have been implemented for backpropagation include adaptive gradient, conjugate gradient descent, Kalman filter, Levenberg–Marquardt, quasi-Newton, and quick propagation, among others. The choice of learning rule is not trivial and can greatly influence model performance and training convergence efficiency. The evolution of learning rule algorithms is progressing rapidly, and the interested reader is encouraged to see Ripley (1996).

Depending on the learning rule chosen, specification of a training regime typically involves setting six different parameters:

1. *Learn count*, also called training schedule, is a schedule that specifies when learning rates and momentum terms are reduced as training progresses. At different stages of learning, smaller changes in the connection weight matrix are needed. Learn count specifies when in training the learning rate and momentum terms are reduced.

2. *Temperature*, also called simulated annealing, refers to random noise added to the connection weight updates under some learning rules. Addition of random noise to the training data set can facilitate learning and generalization from training patterns to test patterns, especially with high noise data. Higher values introduce more random noise, which can be appropriate for some modeling problems. Simulated annealing is used to prevent overtraining and improve generalization in the final model.

3. *Learning rate* is a fractional value that specifies how much the connection weight matrix is modified in response to the backpropagated error received during training at the end of each epoch. If the learning rate is set too high, the connection weights change abruptly, resulting in erratic network behavior evidenced by jagged changes in the RMSE error graph. If the learning rate is set too low, the network converges too slowly or can become trapped in a local minimum. Optimization begins by lowering all rates until the RMSE error plot is smooth, then adjusting the learning rate of each layer until the weight histogram for each layer spreads at the same rate.

4. *Momentum* is a fractional value of the previous weight change that is added to the current matrix update. If the previous solution matrix was moving toward minimum error, momentum creates a directional memory that influences the current solution in the same direction. Like a sled moving downhill, the connection weight matrix with properly calibrated momentum can slide up and over depressions in the local error surface and continue descending toward the global minimum. During early training, adjustments in the range of 0 to .1 can facilitate learning. As RMSE error declines,

incrementally smaller momentum values are used to ensure that the matrix does not pass the minimum error solution.

5. *Error tolerance* is a threshold value that specifies the magnitude of the difference between actual and predicted output required to propagate an error term back through the network. In the latter stages of training, a network may have learned all but one or two remaining patterns. At this point, raising the error tolerance and continuing training eliminate weight updates resulting from small errors and focus the gradient descent algorithm on large errors, presumably associated with the few remaining unknown patterns.

6. *Jogging the current weight matrix* is another option available during training under several different ANN programs. It is a technique for pushing the matrix out of a local minimum to continue descent. When the RMS error graph has stopped descending and all other parameters appear optimal, training is suspended and all connection weights are "tweaked" by adding very small random numbers to all weight values simultaneously. If the current matrix is trapped in a local minimum, jogging the weights as described "pushes" the matrix sideways on the error slope. Occasionally this results in extraction from the local minimum, and the gradient descent can continue.

An important factor in selecting a specific learning rule requires some understanding of how individual neurons process inputs to outputs. Preprocessing the data with exploratory analysis to identify possible nonlinearity in the data is useful for selecting the learning rule (network paradigm) and neuron configuration that are appropriate for modeling a specific data set. A critical consideration is the type of transfer function used by the neural network learning rule.

Types of Transfer Functions

In general, transfer functions are either linear or nonlinear. The output of a linear neuron like Rosenblatt's perceptron is a linear function of the activation value. The activation value is simply multiplied by the gain to derive the output. Linear transfer functions are not widely used because many problems cannot be adequately represented by multiplication. The perceptron used a linear threshold transfer function, shown in Figure 5.3, in which the output is a constant multiple of the input over some range. Below that range, the activation value is 0, above that range, +1.

Because of the thresholding, linear threshold transfer functions are nonlinear. They are not commonly used because a derivative cannot be calculated with linear thresholding and therefore cannot be used for backpropagation-type networks. Linear thresholding was found to limit single-layer perceptron networks learning to problems that are linearly separable and, as a result, is of limited value in most real-world applications (Minsky & Papert, 1969).

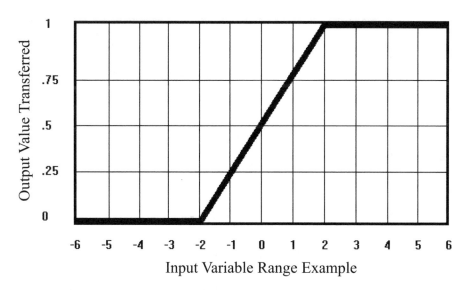

Figure 5.3. Linear threshold function with .25 gain.

The most commonly applied transfer function is the sigmoid function, shown in Figure 5.4. Also called a semilinear or squashing function, the sigmoid function and its derivatives are a continuous, monotonic function of the input that asymptotically approaches both high and low values. At the center point, gain is directly proportional to the derivative, whereas at high and low gain, the sigmoid is almost a step function. The sigmoid

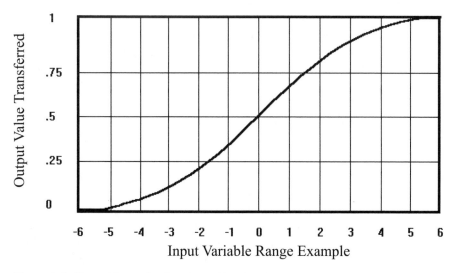

Figure 5.4. Sigmoid transfer function with .25 gain.

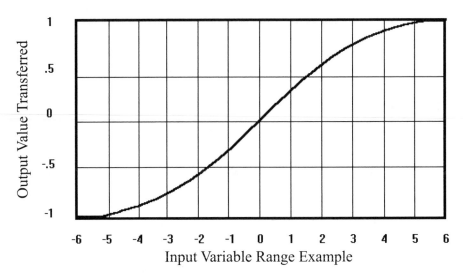

Figure 5.5. Hyperbolic tangent function with .5 gain.

derivative exhibits a Gaussian distribution and results in a continuous output between 0 and 1. The sigmoid and its cousin, the hyperbolic tangent transfer function, work particularly well with backpropagation neural networks because a derivative error value can be calculated for the continuous range of the activation function.

The hyperbolic transfer function, shown in Figure 5.5, also produces continuous, monotonic output and a Gaussian derivative but is bounded by −1 and 1, with 0 at the center point. Other neural transfer functions include the hard limit–step, staircase, Gaussian, threshold exponential, exponential distribution, ratio polynomial, pulse-coded, and competitive signal transfer functions. For more information about neural network transfer functions, see Kosko (1992). Sigmoid and hyperbolic transfer functions are the most commonly used transfers in backpropagation as they are well suited to modeling nonlinearity (Ripley, 1996; Swingler, 1996).

Issue 5: Quantitative Evaluation of Solution Quality

Once training is completed, it is necessary to evaluate the quality of the solution that the neural network has provided. There are several quantitative metrics to accomplish this objective. First, it is essential that test data be run through the network by applying weights generated in training to new cases. The ANN will then generate predicted outcomes that can be compared against known values in the criterion variable. There is always some loss in predictive accuracy between training and test data, and this is to be expected. It is not an indication of poor training. A large drop in predictive accuracy with test data, however, is a clear indication that the network was overtrained.

Overtraining requires retraining of the network with more careful attention to the stopping point. If RMSE error (overall error) is being used as a training criterion, it is helpful to pay careful attention to the point in the curve where error flattens out and additional training cycles do not lead to additional reduction in error. That is a good point to consider ending training.

It is also helpful to compare the results of the ANN with those from conventional statistical analyses. If the criterion is continuous, it is possible to compute the explained variance from the neural network by computing the correlation between actual and observed values for both test and training data. The ANN will usually outperform conventional statistics on both training and test data if nonlinearity is present in the data (Somers, 2001). Similarly, for categorical criterion variables, the percentage correctly classi-fied both within groups and for the total sample can be compared for analyses conducted with a neural network and conventional statistics (see Somers, 1999). Again, if nonlinearity is present, the neural network should outper-form conventional analyses on both test and training data. These analyses are useful in assessing the quality of the solution provided by a neural network, thereby providing some confidence that the results are stable and generalizable.

Issue 6: Qualitative Evaluation of Solution Quality

In addition to being stable and generalizable, it is also important for the solution generated by a neural network to be meaningful. That is, researchers using neural networks face the challenge of explaining why a neural network has produced superior results. The most effective way to address this issue is to conduct sensitivity analyses that map relationships between criterion and predictor variables (StatSoft, Inc., 2002). By examin-ing graphical relationships expressed as a response surface (Edwards & Parry, 1993), one can gain insights into how predictor and criterion variables are related; in other words, disentangle and interpret patterns of nonlinearity.

Some of the relationships generated by ANNs might be counterintu-itive or might require thinking differently about a topic area in organizational research. However, an explanation for the pattern of relationships generated by the ANN is important. Although this task can be challenging, it ought to be possible. In those few cases in which the neural network generates uninterpretable or confused findings that defy logic or explanation, we suggest that retraining is in order.

NEURAL NETWORKS AND MULTIVARIATE STATISTICS IN ORGANIZATIONAL RESEARCH

Because ANNs and conventional multivariate statistical methods are well suited to testing the same hypothesis or studying the same problem (e.g., prediction, classification), it is common and useful to analyze the same data with both techniques (Somers, 1999). It is also possible and useful to compare their relative performance with common metrics. Table 5.1 is intended to serve as a guide for researchers in designing analyses that include conventional multivariate statistics and ANNs.

INTERPRETING NEURAL NETWORK BEHAVIOR USING GRAPHICS

The lattice of connection weights in a trained neural network is not directly interpretable. Instead, the analyst must use other procedures to evaluate and interpret the model. He or she can apply sensitivity analysis, information theoretic techniques, and interaction detection. Data visualization using graphical analysis is also quite useful.

Although a computer can calculate in a large number of dimensions, humans cannot easily comprehend more than four dimensions (length, width, depth, and time). Even with this limitation, we can begin to understand the behavior of a neural model using three-dimensional wire-frame graphs, scatter plots, and surface response graphs of the sample data. By graphing all permutations of each independent variable with every other independent variable on the dependent variable, a visual map of the functions and interactions being modeled is created. Paying particular attention to those inputs with the highest sensitivity on the criterion can provide useful insights for interpreting model behavior.

The concept of an energy surface was introduced in chapter 3 (see the discussion of Figure 3.5). Hidden patterns in the data appear as protrusions and basins underneath a sheet draped over the error surface of the data. During training, gradient descent activity burrows a trajectory beginning with a computational problem and ending with a computational solution. Likened to a ball bearing rolling downhill, the computational solution comes to rest when the network converges in a fixed point of equilibrium (Kosko, 1992). As mentioned earlier, convergence can occur at the true global minima, but it can also occur when equilibrium is reached in a local minimum error that is not the lowest error solution. By adjusting the learning rate and momentum term during different training runs, it is often possible to decide with confidence that the global minimum has been reached (Jacobs, 1988).

TABLE 5.1
Statistical Methods Similar in Application to Different Types of Neural Networks

Problem	Multivariate statistical method	Neural computing paradigm	Performance metrics
Prediction and explanation	OLS regression Moderated OLS regression	Feed-forward with backpropagation of error	*Overall model fit* R^2 Computed by software in OLS regression Computed by correlating predicted and actual values with test and training data for neural networks. This is not done automatically by most ANN software. *Relative influence of predictors* Beta weight: computed by software in OLS regression. Sensitivity analysis: expressed as percentage change in criterion on the basis of percentage change in predictor holding other model variables constant.
Classification	Logistic regression discriminant analysis	Radial basis function Learning vector quantization	*Model fit* Total percentage correctly classified. Percentage correctly classified by group.
Clustering	*k*-means clustering Hierarchical clustering	Self-organizing maps	*Model efficacy* Number and quality of clusters extracted. Differences in profiling variables across clusters using post hoc analysis of variance.

Note. OLS = ordinary least squares. ANN = artificial neural network.

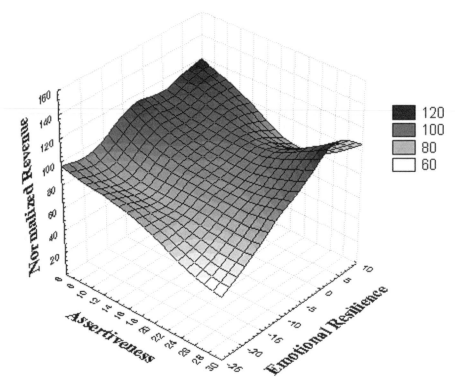

Figure 5.6. Example of two psychological scales used in employment testing plotted on a criterion measure to illustrate nonlinearity and interactivity in three dimensions.

Mapping the error surface is useful for understanding training progression to the global minima. It is also useful to graph independent and dependent variables in a similar way as an aid to understanding nonlinearity and interactivity in the sample data.

One useful convention is to always place the dependent variable on the z-axis (the vertical axis) while assigning two independent variables at a time to the x-axis and y-axis. Such a graph will reveal how these two input variables relate to the dependent variable and to each other. Figure 5.6 is an example of a three-dimensional surface graph of sales productivity (the dependent variable) on the vertical z-axis, plotted against two assessment scales: assertiveness (on the horizontal left axis) and emotional resilience (on the horizontal right axis). The graph indicates that, in this concurrent sample, low assertiveness and emotional resilience scorers also had average to low sales production. Employees scoring high on assertiveness and low on emotional resilience sold the least. Highly assertive staff with moderately high resilience scores sold at the top of the range as did those scoring low on assertiveness but with high emotional resilience. Visual inspection of interaction surfaces can yield insights into the predictor-criterion relationships modeled by a trained neural network. A more detailed example of this technique is described in chapter 7.

This chapter's general guide to using neural networks is intended to provide introductory information needed to begin using ANNs for research. As with all research in any field, knowing what has already been done can increase the efficiency and usefulness of our own research.

II
APPLICATIONS

6

STATISTICS, NEURAL NETWORKS, AND BEHAVIORAL RESEARCH

The first commercially available neural network simulators for personal computers appeared in the market in 1987 and were not well received because of limitations in design and capability (Lawrence, 1993). Today, however, there are dozens of software vendors offering neural network programs to solve a variety of business and scientific problems. One computer science textbook describes 63 different private and public domain neural network programs, and new products continue to emerge (Medsker & Liebowitz, 1994). The availability of better software facilitates experimentation and research with these procedures but does not provide much guidance for behavioral scientists in organizations. Most neural net research has emerged from the physical sciences (Medsker & Liebowitz, 1994). Social science research involving neural network applications are mostly from economics, finance, and neuroscience.

In his excellent introduction to neural networks written for social scientists, Garson (1998) assembled references on 95 studies using neural network analysis from the literatures of business, economics, sociology, political science, and psychology. Of 34 citations from business and economics, only 4 studies involved behavioral analysis in organizations. In sociology, 3 of 9 studies could be considered to have an organizational context. In political science research citations, only 1 of the 7 studies involved organizational behavior. In psychology, 5 of 45 studies came from industrial/organizational psychology.

We have both used neural networks for some time in academic and applied research and follow the literature on this subject. This chapter is our attempt to bring together the admittedly sparse research literature describing behavioral research with neural networks in organizations. We acknowledge that this review is not exhaustive and that newer research not yet published will have been missed for this text.

We first discuss neural network applications as they compare to statistical methods in classification and prediction. Then we present a summary of published and unpublished behavioral research using neural processors in organizational contexts. Our hope is to encourage those who are interested in applying neural network analysis in organizations and who seek to understand what has already been done.

NEURAL NETWORKS AND STATISTICS

As noted previously, neural networks are a class of statistical procedures. A single- or two-layer neural network with a linear transfer function is geometrically (if not computationally) equivalent to multiple linear regression. A single- or two-layer network with a nonlinear transfer function (sigmoidal or hyperbolic tangent) is equivalent to logistic or nonlinear multiple regression. When a hidden layer is added, the resulting neural network can be thought of as a multiple nested logistic regression or as a special case of stochastic approximation (White, 1989a).

In conventional multivariate modeling, the analyst specifies the objective function on the basis of systematic hypothesis testing, whereas neural network modeling applies a fluid medium (modifiable connection weights) to simulate functional relationships captured in sample data using error feedback. It is this capacity to model complex relationships without an a priori mathematical description of the expected pattern function that seems to give neural modeling an advantage for analyzing certain kinds of data.

Within the field of business administration, the disciplines of finance and operations research demonstrated the earliest interest in neural networks. One of the first systematic comparisons of the performance of neural networks and multivariate statistical methods was published by Dutta and Shekhar (1988). For this research, they trained a series of backpropagation neural networks with different architectures to predict corporate bond ratings using nine orthogonal measures of corporate performance and one subjective rating of the company's future prospects. They then developed two regression models using the same independent–dependent variable data set.

At the time of the research, multiple regression was known to be less than satisfactory for the prediction of bond ratings (Caudill, 1990), and the regression models derived for the research were comparable in predictive accuracy with other regression-based attempts. On the training data, the regression models predicted bond ratings correctly about 63% to 67% of the time. The neural networks predicted ratings with an accuracy of 80% to 92%. When compared with the testing data, regression accuracy held at about 65%, and neural accuracy fell to 77% to 82%.

The researchers noted that the total squared error for the regression models tended to be a full order of magnitude greater than that of the neural networks. Furthermore, incorrect regression predictions tended to be large magnitude errors, missing the correct rating by two or more levels. In contrast, incorrect neural predictions were always plus or minus one rating away from the correct rating.

Dutta and Shekhar (1988) found little difference in performance between the various network architectures. The addition of more than one hidden layer had little effect on network performance. Additional middle layers are typically used to extract higher orders of abstraction from the data, and they concluded that for this particular problem, one middle layer was sufficient. The number of hidden neurons could also be varied without significantly affecting network performance.

A similar study described a series of experiments designed to determine the effects of variation in network architecture on bond rating prediction and compared network performance with linear discriminant analysis. Surkan and Singleton (1990) found neural networks with single and multiple hidden layers superior to linear discriminant functions in that application. They also found that the number of hidden neurons in a hidden layer could be varied over a wide range without impairing network performance. Unlike the previous research, however, this study found improvements in performance by adding an additional hidden layer.

Other research, from a variety of disciplines, comparing neural networks with multivariate linear regression and discriminant analysis tends to support the conclusion that the neural approach to classification and prediction is more accurate (Lapedes & Farber, 1987; Rakes, Kohers, Slade, & Rees, 1990; Tang, Almeida, & Fishwick, 1990; Yoon, Swales, & Margavio, 1993). Empirical comparisons of the relative performance of neural networks with nonlinear statistical procedures indicate that neural network performance is either comparable or slightly better, depending on the modeling problem, the data used, and the evaluation metric.

Nam and Prybutok (1992) used simulated data to empirically compare the performance of a neural model with that of a linear discriminant function and a quadratic discriminant function in a two-group classification problem. The three models were tested on populations of different size, variance, and dispersion. This research indicated that the neural approach was slightly more accurate than the linear discriminant function and slightly less accurate than the quadratic function.

In the field of marketing, Dispenza and Dasgupta (1992) compared the results of a backpropagation network, a logistic regression model, and linear discriminant analysis in the prediction of surveyed versus actual buying behavior of specific investment vehicles. In this research, the backpropagation and logistic models performed equally well, and both were more accurate than the discriminant model.

In political science, Schrodt (1991) compared a backpropagation neural network with a linear discriminant model, a rule-based classification tree (an expert system shell called ID3), and a multinomial logit (nonlinear maximum likelihood) model to assess regularities in international political behavior. The neural and logit models were significantly more accurate than the expert system and the linear model. Results with the logit model were approximately equal to those of the neural network.

Another political scientist (Garson, 1991a) compared a backpropagation network, a rule-based expert system (ID3), multiple linear regression, logistic regression, effects analysis, path analysis, and linear discriminant analysis to classify the immediate causes of voting decisions. In this research, backpropagation was found to be more accurate than all other models, even in the presence of noisy and missing data.

A summary of 42 studies comparing neural networks with statistical measures in operations research suggests that neural networks usually out-predicted statistical procedures (Sharda & Patil, 1992). Comparisons included discriminant analysis, Box–Jenkins methodology, logistic regression, linear binary, and multiple regression. In 30 (71%) of the 42 studies, neural networks showed better performance than statistical measures, equal performance in 5 (12%) of the studies, and inferior prediction in 7 (17%) of the studies reported. Most of the results were based on only one training and validation sample and came from unpublished applied research in industry.

Walker and Milne (2005) conducted four experiments comparing linear and nonlinear regression with multilayer perceptron (MLP) networks using constructed linear and nonlinear data sets, real meteorological data, and real behavioral data. The mean r for linear regression and a single-neuron hidden layer network (the simplest possible MLP architecture) was .91, with identical correlations on development and test data for both models. On the constructed nonlinear data, a fitted polynomial regression obtained a mean r of .67 on development and test samples. The mean r for the MLP was .70 on the development sample and .66 on the test sample. The authors interpreted these findings as showing comparable performance for regression and MLP on both constructed data sets.

With the meteorological data, none of the regression models produced a statistically significant fit to the data. The linear regression mean r value obtained was .04, and the best third-order polynomial correlation was .33 (almost significant at $p = .08$). The MLP obtained a significant mean r of .48; it is interesting to note that a three-neuron single hidden layer network performed as well as a 60-unit hidden layer network that used an automated regularization procedure (Westbury et al., 2003) to avoid overtraining.

On the behavioral data, which were described as fairly linear, regression mean r on the development sample was .69, falling to .42 on the test data set. For the MLP models, mean r on both samples were .68, declining to .62. Walker and Milne (2005) concluded that "this demonstration has again shown that NNR (neural network regression) is as good as multiple regression at modeling a fairly linear data set and is better at generalizing this model to further data" (p. 33).

This brings to mind an important point about comparing alternative modeling approaches. Comparing the efficacy of different methodologies using the same data makes several assumptions that should, at a minimum, be acknowledged and, if possible, addressed in the research design. First, the assumption that a valid comparison can be made between two or more models developed using different methods because they were developed with identical data may be defensible but is not absolute. Because different modeling procedures have different strengths and weakness, any one data set may have characteristics better suited to a particular modeling approach. Therefore, a single comparative analysis using one data set could be compromised if the characteristics of that particular data are more congruent with the modeling advantages of one of the approaches being evaluated.

Second, such comparisons assume that the full capabilities of each generic procedure are manifest in the specific models developed for that comparison. In theory, a perfect methodological comparison would ensure that the objects of comparison are maximally representative of their class. Although conceptually elegant, this ideal does not exist in the real world of model development. The performance of any statistical model is to some extent limited by the skill, judgment, and persistence of the model developer. Furthermore, it is the rare analyst who exhibits equal mastery of multiple complex modeling procedures. Therefore, model comparison studies should ideally use multiple model developers of comparable skill to develop competitive models using multiple identical data sets that are evaluated independently with metrics specified in advance. When several of these projects have been published, we will have a preponderance of evidence to consider as we evaluate and choose appropriate methods for specific research problems. Walker and Milne's (2005) research comes close to this ideal and begs for replication.

It may be too early in the research history of neural networks to generalize about the superiority or inferiority of sophisticated nonlinear statistical procedures over neural networks and vice versa. Because both sets of procedures have advantages and disadvantages, it is much more likely that the two approaches are complementary and problem specific. Additional research is needed on the appropriate selection of modeling tools vis-à-vis neural network and conventional modeling approaches. This is especially important in organizational science, in which research with neural networks is at an early stage.

NEURAL NETWORKS AND BEHAVIORAL PREDICTION IN ORGANIZATIONS

According to one popular neural network vendor, neural programs are currently being used in numerous applications related to behavioral prediction. These include the following: psychiatric diagnosis and treatment outcome prediction, employee selection using weighted application blanks, college admission application screening, credit application screening, sales prospect selection, security risk profiling, mental testing, drug screening, selection of criminal investigation targets, predicting parolee recidivism, personnel profiling, and employee retention (Ward Systems Group, Inc., 1993).

In the field of clinical psychology, Lykins and Chance (1992) compared the performance of a stepwise regression model with that of three variants of backpropagation in classifying participants on a survey-based criterion designed to assess risk of contracting HIV/AIDS. Unlike the research mentioned earlier, which used dichotomous and nominal dependent variables, the four models predicted a continuous criterion score. Model performance was measured by mean correlation with the criterion and mean absolute error obtained in 10 repetitive trials. Results are shown in Table 6.1.

TABLE 6.1
Comparison of Neural and Regression Model Prediction Results on a
Continuous Criterion Variable

Predictive model	Mean correlation	Mean error
Extended-delta-bar-delta network	.793 ($p = .012$)	18.072 ($p = .006$)
Functional links network	.8 ($p = .003$)	18.03 ($p = .003$)
Fast backpropagation network	.774 ($p = .126$)	18.316 ($p = .001$)
Regression	.743	20.732

Note. From Lykins and Chance (1992).

A priori comparisons between each neural model result and the regression result revealed that, except for the quick backpropagation network, the neural models obtained significant improvement over regression in mean correlation with the criterion. All differences in mean absolute error were significant and favored the neural models. These findings were interpreted as evidence of superior predictive accuracy of the neural models over the multiple regression model.

Marshall and English (2000) demonstrated that neural methods classified at-risk children on the basis of 37 risk factors using Washington State Child Protective Services risk assessment data better than both linear and logistic multiple regression models. The authors posited,

> The improvement in case prediction and classification accuracy is attributed to the superiority of neural networks for modeling nonlinear relationships between interacting variables; in this respect the mathematical framework of neural networks is a better approximation to the actual process of human decision making than linear, main effects regression. (Marshall & English, 2000, p. 102)

In the field of organizational psychology, the earliest neural network research to be published in a peer-reviewed scientific journal was J. M. Collins and Clark's 1993 article in *Personnel Psychology*. The classification accuracy of neural networks was compared with that of linear discriminant regression on a set of two group classification problems. The first comparison involved determining group membership from total quality management team effectiveness ratings data ($N = 81$). The second involved classifying participants from a study of white-collar criminals using personality trait scores to determine whether they were incarcerated or not ($N = 649$). A third analysis was made using "degraded" data, in which random fields from different variables in the model development data from the second study were deleted to increase "noise" to measure model performance degradation when input variables are characterized by faulty or missing data.

Linear regression was more efficient than the neural networks developed from the small sample comparison. On both of the larger sample comparisons, the neural models were found to be more accurate than the linear discriminant function. In addition, neural model performance showed graceful decrement under conditions of noisy data, supporting the utility of neural methods with missing and noisy data, which is not unusual in applied settings.

In another study of employee turnover, two different types of neural networks (MLP and learning vector quantization) were found to be considerably more accurate than logistic regression in the classification of stayers versus leavers. Somers (1999) noted that neural networks were able to represent nonlinear relationships in the data that are relevant for theory development.

In the employee selection area, another study compared neural networks with linear discriminant analysis in the selection of surgical residents using 36 biographical input variables (Aggarwal, Travers, & Scott-Conner, 2000). MLPs were shown to result in better group separation than stepwise discriminant analysis using paired t tests on 30 different samples. Mean separation accuracy for the neural models averaged 12.9% higher than discriminant analysis models.

Using predictor–criterion matched cases from a predictive sample of hourly workers, Ostberg (2005) compared radial basis function (RBF) and MLP neural networks, classification trees, and multivariate linear regression on prediction accuracy of a continuous tenure variable and two dichotomous classification variables of termination status (voluntary or involuntary separation and eligible or not eligible for rehire). MLPs and regression performed similarly on prediction of tenure, both outperforming the RBF network and classification tree models. The MLP model classified termination variables slightly more accurately than regression at lower selection rates but was equivalent at higher selection rates matching the actual distribution of observed values. The RBF network performed similarly to both on one dichotomous variable (voluntary separation) but not the other (rehire eligibility). Classification trees performed worst in all comparisons.

The studies previously referenced support the use of neural networks for solving classification problems traditionally addressed with discriminant and cluster analysis. Other studies have compared the predictive capabilities of trained neural networks with that of linear and nonlinear multiple regression models.

Using normalized annual sales data as a criterion and various scalar values from the Guilford–Zimmerman Temperament Survey, the Differential Factors Opinion Questionnaire, and several custom biodata measures as predictor variables, Scarborough (1995) compared the ranking accuracy of 36 neural networks with that of an ordinary least squares (OLS) regression model and a nonlinear polynomial regression model at high and low selection rates ($N = 1,084$). The neural models were more accurate than the OLS model in all cases and as accurate as the nonlinear model using the McNemar test of significant differences.

Stanton, Sederburg, and Smith (2000) compared the performance of a neural model with multiple regression correlation modeling to estimate a continuous variable. In this research, 41 demographic variables were used to predict job satisfaction as measured by the Job in General scale of the Job Descriptive Index. Additional analyses, reminiscent of J. M. Collins and Clark's (1993) study, were conducted to assess model performance decline following random mean substitution of 20% of the input variables in a cross-validation sample.

When compared on sample data that were not used for model development, the backpropagation neural network output obtained a multiple R of .21, compared with the regression R of .185. More significantly, when compared on the degraded data set, the regression model multiple R fell to .028, whereas R for the neural network remained unchanged to three decimal places. Stanton et al. (2000) concluded "The results of the study indicated a clear superiority of neural network performance over MRC [multiple regression correlation] when data contain numerous missing values" (p. 12).

The Naval Personnel Research and Development Center in San Diego has been actively experimenting with neural modeling in crew selection since 1991. In a series of unpublished monographs, technical reports, and proceedings, the researchers describe and demonstrate potential applications of neural networks in crew selection. Two early reports provide a description of neural networks and their potential in human resource applications (Dickieson & Gollub, 1992; Sands, 1992). A simulated criterion validation[1] comparing neural methods with linear methods followed (Sands & Wilkins, 1991, 1992). The comparison was then replicated using actual test and attrition data from the U.S. Naval Academy (Dickieson & Wilkins, 1992).

In the simulated criterion validation, linear and nonlinear bivariate distributions of various sample sizes (Ns = 100, 500, and 5,000) were generated. Predictor–criterion pairs were partitioned into development (training) and evaluation (testing) samples in the following percentage ratios (20/80, 50/50, and 60/40) corresponding to each sample size previously discussed. Predictor scores were rank ordered and dichotomized (success or fail) for alternative base rates of .05, .25, .5, and .95. In employee selection, the base rate refers to the percentage of applicants hired who were later successful on the job prior to implementation of the new selection procedure.

Alternative selection ratios were imposed, dividing each sample into selected or not selected groups and allowing each simulated case to be assigned a final criterion value (success or failure). This resulted in the formation of a simulated classification outcome matrix, which was then collapsed into a summary matrix. The actual criterion status of each simulated case (success vs. failure) and selection versus rejection were thus identified.

An OLS linear regression model was developed for each sample and was used to predict criterion scores for each simulated subject. Simulated cases were then rank ordered using the criterion score. Backpropagation

---

[1] For a brief review of criterion validation, see the introduction to chapter 7.

networks (with one input, three hidden, and one output neurons) were then trained uniformly (to 100,000 iterations) on each development sample and tested on each evaluation (holdout) sample.

The proportion of correct decisions made by each model was then compared for each combination of function form, sample size, sample split, base rate, selection ratio, and validity coefficient. The McNemar test was used to assess the significance of differences in predictive accuracy between the two models.

Significant differences were obtained in 62 comparisons ($p < .001$) on the curvilinear data sets. Sixty-one of these favored the neural model over the OLS model. No significant differences were obtained for the linear distributions. Fifty-six of the significant differences were obtained in the largest sample size, 6 in the samples of 500, and none from the smallest sample ($n = 100$). Significant differences did not appear to be related to variation in base rate, selection rate, or sample split.

Neural performance relative to the OLS model increased with sample size. With small samples ($N = 100$), neural and regression models performed equally. With somewhat larger samples ($N = 500$), the neural nets were more accurate in 6 of 240 comparisons. With large samples ($N = 5,000$), the neural model was more accurate in 55 cases, the OLS model was more accurate in 1 case, and the remaining cases showed no significant difference.

It is important to note that uniform network architecture and a set limit of training iterations were used for all networks in the study; in short, no problem-specific network optimization occurred. Even so, in all cases save one, the simple networks performed as well as or outperformed the OLS models, varying only according to sample size and the linearity or nonlinearity of the data. The researchers concluded that neural modeling held considerable promise for applications in selection research and that further research using unsimulated predictor–criterion data was warranted.

The second study made use of admission data (SAT—Verbal, SAT—Quantitative, high school rank, recommendations rating, extracurricular activity score, technical interest score, and career interest score) and attrition data from three classes of the U.S. Naval Academy at Annapolis. A stepwise linear regression model was developed on Class 1 and cross-validated using data from Class 2. The resulting model was then used to predict attrition for Class 3. The correlation between predicted and actual attrition for Class 3 (.0561) became the baseline for comparison with the neural network models. Four backpropagation and two functional link neural networks were created as shown in Table 6.2.

A two-phase cross-validation was used to train the networks. Each net was trained on Class 1 and tested on Class 2 in cycles of 10,000 iterations to an upper limit of 200,000 iterations. These results were used to find the optimum number of training iterations for each network, which was then

TABLE 6.2
Naval Personnel Research and Development Center Experimental Neural
Network Architectures

Network	Type	Neurons in input layer	Neurons in first hidden layer	Neurons in second hidden layer	Neurons in output layer
1	Backprop	7	14	0	1
2	Backprop	7	7	0	1
3	Fun/link	7	7	0	1
4	Fun/link	7	4	3	1
5	Backprop	7	21	0	1
6	Backprop	7	2	0	1

Note. From Dickieson and Wilkins (1992). Backprop = backpropagation. Fun/link = functional link.

cross-validated on Class 3 data. Training was stopped using two criteria: Criterion A, the number of iterations that provided the maximum cross-validation correlation for Class II; and Criterion B, the midpoint of the range of iterations at which the neural correlation exceeded that of the regression model. Correlations between the resulting network's predicted attrition and the actual attrition were then computed. In all cases, using both stopping criteria, the neural network's correlation with actual attrition exceeded that of the regression model as shown in Table 6.3.

Although it is common to report absolute error in comparisons of this nature, the correlation differences obtained are compelling. It is interesting to note that only one network of one type (functional link) was designed with more than one hidden layer, and it obtained a correlation comparable with that of the regression model. These results again supported the use of neural networks as an alternative validation methodology. The researchers conclude by indicating that further research on neural configuration and optimization in behavioral prediction is under way at the Naval Personnel Research and Development Center.

TABLE 6.3
Naval Personnel Research and Development Center Neural Network
Versus Regression Model Results

Network	Regression	Criterion A	Criterion B
1	.0561	.0846	.0806
2	.0561	.0806	.0762
3	.0561	.0854	.0858
4	.0561	.0577	.0577
5	.0561	.0860	.0769
6	.0561	.0657	.0657

Note. From Dickieson and Wilkins (1992).

A third study (Depsey, Folchi, & Sands, 1995) compared OLS regression and neural network predictive models to predict attrition of enlisted personnel. McNemar's test for correlated proportions was used to compare the results of both modeling procedures using age at enlistment, education, test scores, and number of dependents as predictor inputs and success or failure in completion of contracted enlistment as the criterion group assignment. In this study, the neural models performed as well or better than OLS models and quadratic logistic models in 39 of 46 comparisons (85%).

The behavioral studies described in this chapter, as well as those described from other disciplines, provide clear evidence of the utility of neural modeling procedures in social research. Measurement of neural model accuracy mirrored findings from the physical sciences indicating that neural models are generally more accurate than simple linear methods, particularly when the underlying functions are nonlinear or unknown. A consistent pattern of findings also suggests that neural methods compare favorably with sophisticated nonlinear models used to predict continuous, dichotomous, and nominal dependent variables and may generalize to new data better.

Three of the studies reported found that predictive accuracy of neural networks degrades gracefully in the presence of missing and noisy data, again mirroring engineering studies of neural network performance. The property of graceful degradation is particularly salient for certain behavioral prediction applications, such as employee selection, as discussed in the following chapter.

7

USING NEURAL NETWORKS IN
EMPLOYEE SELECTION

Before the early 1990s, the way people found employment had not changed very much for over a century. In Lincoln's time, the common practice was to submit a letter of intent and curriculum vitae to solicit professional employment. Laborers were hired much less formally but no more objectively than the educated workforce. In the United States and Europe, the use of employment application forms became common after World War I, and the use of paper resumes and employment applications continues today.

In the last half of the 20th century, as information technology was applied to almost every organizational task, employee selection was among the last common functions to harness the full capabilities of fast computing. Early computer applications related to recruiting and hiring tended to mirror the preceding paper processes. Computer-based employment tests, automated employment applications, Internet job boards, applicant tracking systems, and hiring-related Web sites accelerated but generally replicated paper-based administrative procedures.

Today networked computers are revolutionizing employee selection. One important new capability is that, for the first time, organizations have the technology to provide statistically informed hiring decision support over computer networks, centralizing, standardizing, and measuring hiring practices in a way that was impossible using paper-based administration. Technology brings other advantages as well. All applicants experience a uniform process and are evaluated on job-related selection criteria with total consistency. Access to job opportunities can be improved because physical proximity and office-hour time constraints do not apply to Internet job seekers. We are convinced that automated employment application processing is likely to become a standard organizational practice because the economic and scientific advantages of these systems are significant and measurable (Autor & Scarborough, 2004; Handler & Hunt, 2003; S. Hunt et al., 2004; Scarborough, 2002; Yerex, 2005).

Internet-based hiring systems allow low-cost, large-sample data capture for employee selection validation research. When applicant processing is coupled to a hiring decision support system and linked to employee performance databases, a closed-loop system is created. All data elements of selection research are captured organically (in the normal course of hiring and termination activity) and used to populate a comprehensive data warehouse of applicant and employee records. Data-mining procedures, including the use of artificial neural networks, allow validation modeling of inexpensive performance criterion data (payroll, safety, sales productivity, etc.), which are often linked to measures of organizational performance. In this data-rich environment, other opportunities for behavioral research are created that transcend and supplement the organizational objective of hiring better employees efficiently.

SCIENTIFIC EMPLOYEE SELECTION

Organizational use of scientific methods for the selection and placement of employees and soldiers was first described in the United States shortly after the turn of the 20th century (Munsterberg, 1913; Yerkes, 1921). These early works and much subsequent research were based on the recognition that people differ in ways that have profound and measurable effects on how well they adjust to and perform in different occupational roles.

Given that organizations are made up of people acting in concert to achieve common goals, organizational effectiveness is inseparable from the individual effectiveness of the membership. Validation of employee selection procedures is the systematic investigation of how individual differences relate to job effectiveness and the application of these relationships for improving employee selection.

Employee selection research attempts to link quantified characteristics of people, called predictors,[1] with measures of individual job effectiveness,

---

[1] Typical predictive variables used in employee selection research include education, work experience, psychological test scores, and other job-related information collected from or about applicants that can be quantified or classified.

called criteria.[2] The central statistic describing this linkage is the Pearson product–moment correlation coefficient, which in this context is also called a *validity coefficient*. To the extent that a predictor test score or similar measure correlates with a job-related criterion, the test is said to be valid or useful.

The logic of criterion-related validity holds that predictor–criterion correlations observed among current and former workers (a validation sample population) will also be observed in the population of future workers. Summarizing these associations in a scoring formula (a model) and measuring applicants in a manner identical to that used to measure the validation sample provide a statistically reliable comparison of the applicant with the validation sample. If the measured characteristics of an applicant are similar to those of better workers, the statistical model should provide an index of this similarity expressed in a value that supports a hiring decision. The converse is also true.

Consistent use of criterion valid employee selection has been shown to increase both individual and organizational effectiveness (Schmidt & Hunter, 1998). Criterion validation procedures are widely supported in the scientific literature and in legislation governing employment practices in the United States and many other countries (Equal Employment Opportunity Commission et al., 1978; Guion, 1998).

STATISTICAL MODELS OF CRITERION VALIDITY

The generally accepted method for establishing the criterion validity of a selection test or other standardized selection procedure requires informed theory building and hypothesis testing that seek to confirm or reject the presence of a functional relationship between a set of independent predictor variables and a dependent criterion variable(s). This is ordinarily expressed as

$$Y = f(X_1, X_2, \ldots X_n),$$

where Y is the criterion variable to be predicted and X is a variable (or set of variables) hypothesized to predict Y.

Because human traits and work behaviors are complex, criterion-related validity improves as additional valid predictors are added that are not intercorrelated to a high degree. The standard method of validation model development is to "identify predictors that meet these requirements, score

---

[2] Criterion measures of job effectiveness can include performance ratings by supervisors, productivity measures, length of service, promotions, demotions, pay changes, commendations, disciplinary records, and other quantifiable metrics of job behaviors that support or detract from organizational performance.

TABLE 7.1
A Job–Person Characteristics Matrix

	PC_1	PC_2	PC_3
JC_1	$r_{1,1}$	$r_{1,2}$	$r_{1,3}$
JC_2	$r_{2,1}$	$r_{2,2}$	$r_{2,3}$
JC_3	$r_{3,1}$	$r_{3,2}$	$r_{3,3}$

Note. From *Integrating the Organization: A Social Psychological Analysis*, by H. L. Fromkin and J. J. Sherwood (Eds.), 1974, p. 2. Copyright 1974 by the Free Press, a division of Macmillan, Inc. Reprinted with permission.

them, weight the scores according to a specified rule, and sum the weighted scores. Such a procedure simultaneously considers all predictors and yields a linear, additive composite score" (Guion 1992, p. 367).

By using multiple regression, individual predictor values can be weighted to maximize the correlation of the composite score with the criteria. Calculation of the validity coefficient becomes a multivariate regression function similar to the following:

$$Y' = b_0 + b_1X_1 + b_2X_2 \ldots b_nX_n + e,$$

where Y' is the estimated criterion variable, $X_1 \ldots X_n$ are predictor variables, b_0 is the intercept, b_1, b_2, $\ldots b_n$ are the least squares estimate or slope of each predictor within the sampled function, and e is an error term to account for deviation from the model. Nonlinearities can be represented using polynomials, such as square, quadratic, step, and other functions, to maximize model fit although the use of nonlinearities is not a routine practice (Guion, 1998).

NEURAL NETWORKS AND CRITERION VALIDATION

One of the more useful frameworks for visualizing employee selection research designs was proposed by Dunnette (1963). In the job–person characteristics matrix, predictor variables, correlations (r), or other descriptive statistics and data are presented for each predictor–criterion pair in a matrix format, with person characteristics (predictor vectors $PC_{1,2,3}$) identified in each column and job characteristics (criterion vectors, $JC_{1,2,3}$) in each row, as shown in Table 7.1.

The predictor–criterion pairing, in which predictor (input) variables are mapped through hypothesis testing and model building to specific performance measures (output), is analogous to the input and output processing of a neural network. There are several notable differences between the two modeling approaches.

Under the job–person characteristics approach, each predictor variable is linked theoretically to a corresponding feature of the job and an associated criterion measure. Each hypothesized functional relationship is tested and either accepted for use in a summary model or rejected if support for the hypothesized predictor–criterion pairing is lacking. The resulting validation model is thus a combination of those predictive associations supported by individually tested confirmation of effect and significance. This well-reasoned approach to behavioral research is tailor made for construction of fully specified linear and nonlinear validation models.

NEURAL VALIDATION MODELING

As stated previously, neural modeling does not provide individual hypothesis confirmation of predictor–criterion pairings. Assumptions of predictor independence, linearity, normality, or additivity are unnecessary. Also, as described in the previous chapter, there is a growing body of evidence that neural network models are able to model behavioral data accurately, generalize to new data well, and tolerate noisy data better than regression procedures commonly used for scoring predictor content.

Even though a neural modeling approach does not require theoretical specification, the use of a neural network for behavioral prediction increases the importance of rigorous validation methodology. Job analysis remains central to predictor construct identification and development. Careful attention to criterion fidelity will pay dividends in final model performance and generalization. Knowledge of theoretically useful predictor–criterion associations, reliable construct measurement and scaling, preanalytic power analysis, and other features of well-structured validation research are as critical to neural validation modeling as they are to conventional modeling approaches. Finally, neural selection models can be studied and interpreted for theoretical congruence.

WHY USE NEURAL NETWORKS FOR EMPLOYEE SELECTION?

If traditional methods have been shown to be effective for criterion validation modeling and both approaches use similar data collection and research design strategies, when does using a neural network make sense? Echoing themes introduced in chapter 1, the following discussion is intended to guide researchers in evaluating neural network modeling for criterion validation projects. In general, when one or more of the following conditions are present in an applied selection research project, neural network modeling should be considered.

When predictor–criterion fidelity is low and unexplained variance is large

Decades of employee selection research have given industrial/organizational psychologists many measures of abilities, attitudes, personality, and other intrinsic person characteristics that are useful for occupational placement. Predictor content, however, is only half of the measurement problem. Reliable, theoretically sound predictors are rarely matched to criterion measures of equal quality. Quantitative job analysis, competency modeling, structured performance scaling, and other techniques can improve the theoretical matching of predictors to criteria; however, uncontrolled sources of variance are ever present (Smith, 1976). When unexplained variance remains stubbornly high with traditional modeling procedures, a neural network model may be able to fit the data more accurately.

When the theoretical basis of prediction is ambiguous

Some criterion valid predictors of job effectiveness are based on scientific theories that are still evolving. A good example of this is the use of standardized measures of biographical facts related to life history, work experience, and other information, often referred to as *biodata* (Nickels, 1994). Well-designed biodata predictors can provide robust prediction when validated locally but often do not generalize across multiple work settings, even for similar jobs. Several competing theories have been advanced to explain biodata validity and utility; however, the generalizability problem remains the subject of ongoing debate and research (Mumford, Snell, & Reiter-Palmon, 1994). Ambiguity or absence of a sound theoretical model explaining how and why a predictor set should relate to available criterion measures is, in our opinion, a reasonable methodological justification for applying a neural modeling procedure.

When sample data show high dimensionality, multiple variable types, and complex interaction effects between predictors and do not meet parametric assumptions

Employee selection procedures often capture several different types of predictive information, most of which is not used for behavioral prediction. Employment application biodata, psychometric and attitudinal questionnaire responses, job-related physical capacities, and other measures can be used to improve prediction synergistically. In practice, this rarely occurs because standard multivariate modeling procedures favor uniform variable structure, parsimonious models, and linear estimation.

Employment application biodata is the most common predictive information collected from applicants and usually consists of a mixed bag of variable types. Categories and approximate rankings are common. Even continuous biodata variables show distributional characteristics that rarely fit parametric assumptions. Modeling biodata predictor content using standard multivariate procedures is a complex process fraught with methodological threats to validity from problematic scaling, interaction effects, tenuous criterion fidelity, and other problems. When complexity of available validation data exceeds the efficient representational capacity of standard multivariate modeling, a neural network should be considered.

When operational use of the predictive model requires high fault tolerance

Internet and computer-based employment application processing is becoming a standard practice among large companies. As applicants apply online, low-cost predictor data are entered directly into computer networks for processing and storage. Within seconds, predictor content is passed through validation models, and statistically informed hiring recommendations are e-mailed to hiring managers. Although more research on Internet-based assessment and employee selection programs is needed, recent studies suggest that unproctored online assessments generally retain psychometric integrity and predictive utility (Beaty, Fallon, & Shepherd, 2002; Gosling, Vazire, Srivastava, & John, 2004; Kraut et al., 2004; Ployhart, Weekley, Holtz, & Kemp, 2002; Sinar, Paquet, & Scott, 2002).

Electronic selection procedures are administered by software controls and user-interface design instead of human proctors. The loss of environmental control over unproctored completion of electronic questionnaires simultaneously increases sample size and response pattern variation. Internet applicant populations are in theory unlimited by geographic constraints and show wider linguistic and cultural variation. Differences in education, motivation, reading ability, computing dexterity, and many other factors contribute to response variability. Additional threats to data integrity are inherent to the computer medium. Software glitches, hardware failures, network traffic, and other factors can degrade digital data and further increase the variability of applicant data from online sources.

Recall from chapter 6 the findings of Collins and Clark (1993); Garson (1991a); and Stanton, Sederburg, and Smith (2000) in which data integrity was systematically degraded to compare performance decline between various neural networks and a variety of statistical models. The ability of neural networks to produce reasonable estimates using noisy and missing input variables is a significant advantage over more brittle[3]

---

[3] Brittleness refers to the fault tolerance of a predictive model. Multivariate regression, discriminant, and quadratic model accuracy degrade rapidly or fail when one or more independent variables presented to the model is noise (e.g., a missing value or a random value of unexpected magnitude or valence). Neural networks encode functional relationships across a dispersed connection weight matrix. The effects of missing or unexpected input variables are dispersed within the network, causing degradation of model performance without catastrophic failure.

modeling procedures for processing complex, unrefined data of variable quality in real-time applications.

High fault tolerance and graceful degradation of model accuracy are two properties of neural network models that have speeded their deployment in various engineering applications with high input data variability. Nuclear energy production, refinery control systems, voice and image recognition, and signal processing involving high-dimensional, nonlinear complex streaming data sources were among the first neural network applications (Glatzer, 1992; Schwartz, 1992). In our opinion, a similar technology transfer will occur in real-time processing of behavioral data. Criterion valid neural models in operational use for online employee selection systems are described later in this chapter.

When the measurement environment supports or requires opportunistic validation data mining

Data mining is the growing practice of applying exploratory and con-firmatory analysis to large-scale databases to uncover useful relationships embedded therein (Ye, 2003). Criterion valid models of employee behavior can be developed using data sources created for other purposes. Cost-efficient predictor content can be derived from employment applications and assess-ment records collected via computer networks. On the criterion side, payroll data contain length of service, termination records, promotion or demotion activity, compensation changes, and other data that can be scaled to reflect meaningful performance differences among workers. Other potentially useful sources of performance criteria include records of sales and commission data, unit production, service transactions, accidents and disciplinary records, performance appraisal ratings, and other quantifiable measures of job perfor-mance that can be linked to specific employees for whom matching predictor data are available.

In data mining, very large sample size and very low data acquisition costs are offset by variable data integrity and measurement precision with no experimental control over data collection. Opportunistic data mining is a scavenger's game, and numerous caveats apply. Careful examination and preprocessing of opportunistic validation data should precede any attempt at modeling. Feature selection, that is, choosing the right set of predictor variables, is challenging because such data were collected for purposes other than behavioral research.

No behavioral theory-based judgments went into collecting such data, so it is incumbent on the analyst to ensure, as much as possible, that these harvested measures are not characterized by bias or systemic contamination. We have experience with two types of systemic confounds that apply to any criterion validation modeling project: neural or conventional.

Bias in criterion measures is very well documented (Guion, 1998; Kane & Freeman, 1986; Lawler, 1967; Smith, 1976). Opinion data in the form of performance ratings and other so-called objective measures of employee performance are always subject to systemic sources of error. As stated previously, a neural network will model predictor–criterion mappings accurately. If the procedures used to measure job performance have been influenced by intentional or unintentional illegal bias, a neural model is very likely to replicate that bias in a selection model. Equally important are confounds without legal implication that increase error. There is no substitute for a cautious and thorough examination of criterion measures with an eye for method variance and bias.

In the prediction of length of service, it is important to check input variables for any time-bound relationships among predictors that may not be obvious. Seasonality in hiring patterns can introduce time-bound effects in predictive validation data, as can irregular events such as layoffs, mergers, and reorganizations. Subtle changes in item format or content that occur in early periods and not later can tip off a neural model that a distributional change in the sample data has a temporal element. Location information in growing companies can result in sequential ordering of a sample, which the network will use to fit the observed length of service distribution. Our advice here is to not underestimate the capacity of a neural model to integrate subtle relationships that can be traced to sampling error and not explainable variance. In this type of validation project, characterized by large sample size, noisy predictor and criterion data, minimal theoretical grounding, limited experimental control, and exclusively electronic model processing, a neural network may be the only viable modeling choice. With a conservative approach to analysis and sensitivity to these issues, usable models can be developed; one of these is described later in this chapter.

When evaluating the performance of alternative models

Neural networks can provide a useful benchmark for evaluating other types of models, linear or nonlinear. As mentioned previously, many neural network software programs have utilities for scaling, data cleansing, feature selection, and automated model creation and testing. These tools allow researchers to efficiently create families or *ensembles* of neural networks that vary by architecture, learning rule, convergence conditions, and other parameters. This type of brute force computational attack can provide reasonable initial estimates of model fit that might be obtained using other modeling approaches on a given data set. Other information on the extent of nonlinearity, interaction effects, and generalizability can be gleaned as well.

In addition to exploratory estimates of model fit, the performance of optimized neural models can be compared directly with that of other optimized statistical models. In many instances, a fully specified statistical model that maps the underlying function to a theory-based explanation is required. If neural model fit is significantly better than that of the specified model, this may indicate that the model is incomplete or that some functional relationships are not being represented accurately. The model fit of an optimized neural network that generalizes to independent data reliably can be viewed as a reasonable approximation of the explainable variance in a data set. When a specified formal model approximates the fit of an optimized neural network (or better, an ensemble of neural networks), this can be viewed as one form of corroboration of the specified model.

EMPLOYEE SELECTION NEURAL NETWORKS

This section describes several neural network models trained with criterion validation sample data to estimate a job performance measure that can then be used to inform hiring decisions in the same manner that a traditional linear scoring algorithm would be used. An employee selection network (ESN) is always of the trained feed-forward network type because the sample data include a correct answer (one or more job performance criterion variables) that the network is being trained to estimate.

In each of the neural validation studies described, validation sample data were randomly partitioned into three subsamples: a training set, a test set, and an independent holdout sample. The training data set is used to train the network from an initial randomized state to a converged solution. The test data set, which is not part of the training data, is used during training to assess model learning and generalization. This process suspends training periodically and passes new data from the test data set through the partially trained neural network. The output of these test runs are graphically displayed on a training graph, as explained in chapter 5 and shown in Figure 5.2.

Successful model training is indicated when model accuracy on the test data improves and eventually approximates training set accuracy. When a trained model accurately predicts from training records but fails to perform comparably on test data, overtraining has occurred. Recall from chapter 5 that overtraining refers to "memorization" of the training sample, meaning that the neural network is unable to generalize learning of the essential functional relationships from the training set to data that it has not encountered previously (the test data). When the analyst is satisfied that the newly trained neural model has extracted the essential structural relationships embedded in the training data and that these learned pattern functions also apply to the test data as indicated by comparable model performance, training is complete.

The final test of model generalization can then be executed. This is the purpose of the independent holdout data. By running this third set of nonoverlapping sample data through the trained neural net and comparing model accuracy statistics with those previously obtained for the training and test data sets, an additional confirmation of generalized learning is obtained. Of course, the best and final metrics of model accuracy and generalization are obtained after the model has been put to use in an operational setting to inform real hiring decisions.

An ESN Trained to Estimate Normalized Sales Revenue

The data used to develop this ESN were taken from a national concurrent validation study conducted for a large service organization based in the southwestern United States (Bigby, 1992). A computer-based questionnaire consisting of personality, attitudinal, and biodata predictor content was validated against a normalized measure of revenue production among inbound sales call center agents. A sophisticated nonlinear regression equation was deployed that resulted in a 9% to 11% increase in mean sales productivity among new hires selected using this procedure.

Scarborough (1995) used these archival data to develop 36 neural nets to compare with the deployed proprietary nonlinear model using high and low selection rates. With the McNemar test for significance of change (Conover, 1980), no significant performance differences between the neural models and the proprietary model were observed at $p = .01$. In 70 paired comparisons, the nonlinear model was somewhat better than the networks 42 times; networks were slightly better 20 times; and in 8 of the comparisons the models were equal. Holdout sample correlation between the actual criterion and network estimates ranged from .23 to .27, compared with .33 for the nonlinear model. This early study confirmed previous work demonstrating the feasibility of ESNs but did not show higher accuracy using the neural validation approach.

Neural validation modeling procedures have improved considerably in the past decade. Newer backpropagation algorithms, gains in computation speed, and the skill of scientists using neural networks in this application make it possible to obtain higher validities. To illustrate this increase, the same data set was used to create a new crop of neural models, and the best of these is presented as an example of an ESN constructed using well-designed psychometric instrumentation, rigorous concurrent validation research with good experimental controls, and known outcome utility.

By using linear item-level and scale correlation for initial feature selection followed by nonparametric information theoretic feature selection (Chambless & Scarborough, 2001), a new set of predictor variables was identified. Model development procedures similar to those described in

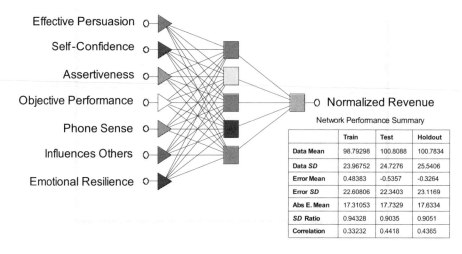

Backprop ESN (7-5-1) Trained to Estimate Sales Agent Productivity

	Train	Test	Holdout
Data Mean	98.79298	100.8088	100.7834
Data SD	23.96752	24.7276	25.5406
Error Mean	0.48383	-0.5357	-0.3264
Error SD	22.60806	22.3403	23.1169
Abs E. Mean	17.31053	17.7329	17.6334
SD Ratio	0.94328	0.9035	0.9051
Correlation	0.33232	0.4418	0.4365

Figure 7.1. Employee selection network (ESN) trained to estimate revenue production of call center agents using personality assessment predictors. *SD* = standard deviation.

chapter 5 produced several sets of networks. The ESN chosen for description was a three-layer backpropagation network with architecture 7:5:1 trained in 600 epochs. The hidden layer was trained using the backpropagation learning rule, and the output layer was trained using conjugate gradient descent (StatSoft, Inc., 2003a). The model, with summary performance statistics, is shown in Figure 7.1.

This model was one of several dozen networks developed that produced validity coefficients above .4 on the independent sample. Twenty-one surface response graphs were produced, one for each combination of predictors with the criterion, two of which are presented here with interpretive comment. In chapter 5 the use of surface response graphs was introduced as a method for representing neural network geometric computation. As an ESN network is trained, each set of predictors is treated as a vector in a hyperspace model that is systematically positioned in relation to the criterion with each training cycle or epoch. In the connection weight matrix, each case vector is mapped to a centroid location in the hyperspace model, and when all vectors have been adequately mapped, prediction accuracy stops improving, indicating convergence.

Psychologists have long recognized that personality and ability measures interact in complex ways. Configural scoring models that quantify these interactions linearly, using some form of banded range scoring, are fairly common and also characterize the predictors developed in this research.

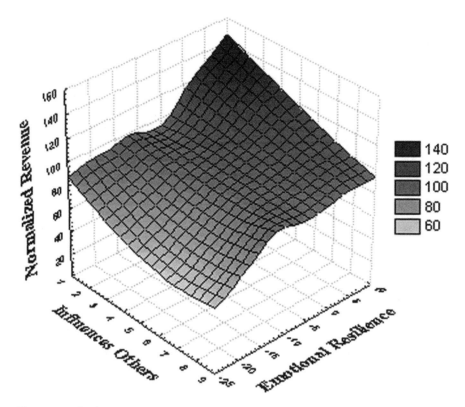

Figure 7.2. Surface response plot showing interaction between two personality scales and a normalized criterion measure with the mean set to 100.

The surface response graph provides an intuitive visualization of how two variables interact. A thorough understanding of the job, the criterion measures, and the predictor content can be used to interpret neural net mapping. In Figure 7.2, two self-report personality scales are plotted in relation to a normalized criterion measure of revenue production with the mean performance set to 100.

The call center employees measured in this study work in a large cube farm hooked up to headsets and computer screens. Incoming call traffic is constant; as one sales call comes to an end, another begins immediately. Agents have no direct control over work volume or personal workspace, often working everyday in a different cube that is shared with other agents working different shifts. Calls and screen activity are monitored by software and supervisor phone taps. Customers, unfettered by social niceties of face-to-face interaction, can be rude and abusive on the phone. The job is stressful; voluntary and involuntary turnover are fairly high. Yet, some agents perform well and even thrive in this really tough job.

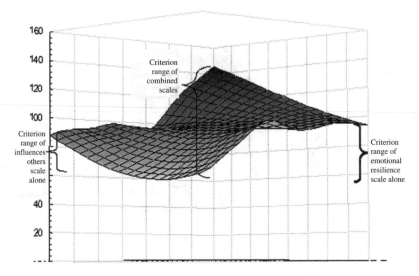

Figure 7.3. Surface response plot showing interaction between two personality scales and a normalized criterion measure tilted to reveal criterion range coverage.

Not surprisingly, people who describe themselves as mentally tough and emotionally well adjusted adapt to this highly monitored work environment characterized by rude customers and frequent rejection better than those who report being sensitive to criticism and subject to moodiness. People who see themselves as capable of influencing others and understanding how to interact with others to get their way also perform better in this sales job. Significantly, people who score high on both of these scales do even better, another theoretically interpretable finding.

Individually, these linearly transformed banded score scales (emotional resilience and influences others) obtain validity coefficients of .23 and .14, respectively. The bivariate distribution of each scale on the criterion can be visualized by rotating the perspective of the same surface response graph as shown in Figure 7.3. Note the much larger criterion space coverage of the combined scales, which interact synergistically to differentiate on the criterion better than either scale alone. Although this kind of synergistic interaction effect can be identified using two-way interaction detection, specification of this and the other interactions in a regression model is complex and time consuming. Consider that this ESN is fitting 21 curvilinear surfaces in this fairly simple six-input model. Replication of this model's behavior using formal specification would require a lengthy series of analyses to detect and model these interactions, assuming the analyst would test for and identify them all. In contrast, this model was one of thousands developed overnight using batch processing. As explained in chapter 1, machine intelligence can do things that humans cannot do. Testing all permutations of

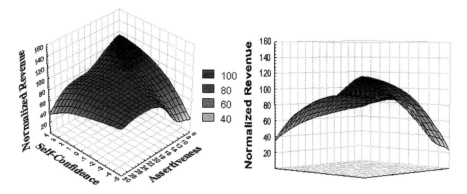

Figure 7.4. Surface response plots showing interaction between two personality scales and a normalized criterion measure.

interactions between all variables in a complex sample is an activity ideally suited to the capabilities of computers but not those of humans.

Surface response analysis will also reveal that some predictor pairings seem to differentiate more effectively within different ranges of the criterion. In this sample, call center staff who measured in the lower range of the assertiveness scale but high in the self-confidence scale showed moderately above-average performance. Low productivity was associated with high self-confidence and high assertiveness. In a service-selling role using voice-only communication, the need to dominate interpersonal communication can get in the way of closing a commercial transaction. Confident communication, combined with willingness to accommodate the customer, allows at least average performance in this job. At the same time, very low productivity was associated with low self-confidence and low assertiveness, indicating that people who accept rejection too easily are not likely to be effective. Note the extreme nonlinearity of the combined scales and the range of criterion coverage extending from the mean (100) downward two standard deviations shown in Figure 7.4.

Assertiveness, in combination with another sales-related scale, effective persuasion, also differentiated in the higher range of performance. The Effective Persuasion scale is developed from keyed responses to an adjective checklist in which participants are instructed to choose from a set of descriptive adjectives (scaled for comparable social desirability) those words that they feel describe them most and least (Bigby, 1992). The effective persuasion scale measures self-reported enjoyment of and personal efficacy in the selling process, reflecting a balance between service and selling.

Low assertiveness and high effective persuasion map vectors two standard deviations above the criterion mean, as shown in Figure 7.5. Both predictors show approximate linearity individually, but in combination,

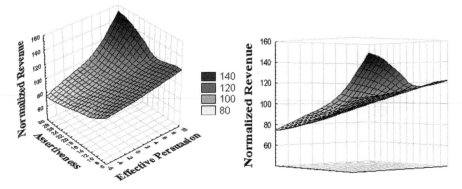

Figure 7.5. Surface response plots showing interaction between two personality scales and a normalized criterion measure.

distinct nonlinearity begins in the mid-range of both variables sloping sharply upward. This graph supports viewing assertiveness as a moderator of selling effectiveness (in this call center setting) with high scores associated with lower performance, particularly in combination with these two other predictors.

Interpretation of neural network model behavior using surface response graphs is one of several procedures for understanding how these models map functional relationships and process individual vectors (cases). Garson (1991a, 1991b, 1998) described two other procedures for interpreting neural network behavior to assign causal inferences, if imperfectly. The first procedure involves partitioning connection weights from each hidden neuron to each output neuron into components associated with each input neuron; the resulting values are the percentages of all output weights attributed to each input variable. These can be interpreted as similar to beta weights in a regression equation to assess relative contribution of each predictor variable to the model solution.

A second approach uses input variable smoothing (introducing a Gaussian noise factor) in generalized regression neural networks and probabilistic neural networks. These architectures allow the analyst to vary the smoothing factor until an input variable is swamped by the noise factor. If model generalization improves, that input variable can be viewed as trivial to model performance. In the opposite case, if model performance degrades as input noise is increased, that input is shown to be critical to model performance (Garson, 1998). Both procedures become unreliable as the number of input variables increases.

Neural network processing occurs in a diffused connection weight medium consisting of thousands of individual connections and weights in a complex lattice that is not easily interpreted. Assigning causal inferences to neural network behaviors remains the subject of ongoing research, and neural analysts have much to be humble about when it comes to explaining how neural modeling procedures arrive at specific estimates. In the applied context of employee selection research, inferences of causality and refinement of behavioral theories may be less important than accurate and fair behavioral prediction of important job-related criteria.

An ESN Trained to Estimate Length of Service

Turnover, the constant replacement of workers exiting an organization, can be a constructive source of organizational renewal as new employees are hired to replace those who leave. In many organizations, however, excessive employee turnover can be a costly impediment to organizational effectiveness. When employees do not stay long enough to repay employer investments in hiring and training, poor employee retention can lead to inferior customer service, reduced productivity, higher payroll expenses, increased absenteeism, and other negative outcomes. Large service-sector companies, such as retailers, food-service operators, hospitality companies, and health care providers who employ large numbers of hourly workers, are particularly hard hit. As such, these organizations have a vested interest in hiring applicants who are more likely to stay on the payroll long enough to contribute to profitability.

Research Background and Source of Data

Beginning in the mid-1990s, a number of small technology companies began providing automated employment and recruiting data processing. These computer service providers automate the collection and processing of employment applications and resumes, establishing a niche in the human capital industry that appears stable a decade later. Data used to develop this ESN came from a client of one such company, which specialized in high-volume processing of hourly employment applications.

This firm provides locally deployed data collection devices and hosted Web sites that allow applicants to enter their employment application, assessment questionnaire responses, and other information directly into a computer network (see Figure 7.6). With this system, applicant data are uploaded, parsed into related segments, processed, and used to produce an employment application and summary hiring report. Within a few minutes of upload, the hiring manager receives a facsimile or e-mail image of the application package containing key information needed to make an hourly employment decision on the spot.

By year-end 2004, over 18,000 units had been deployed across the United States in thousands of retail stores, hotels, restaurants, movie

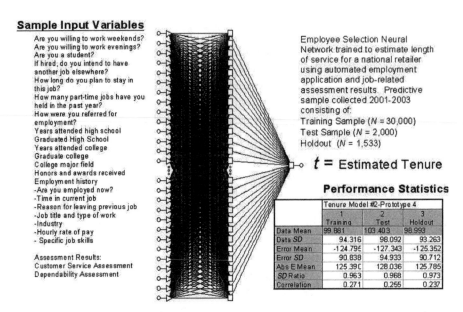

Figure 7.6. Employee selection network trained to estimate tenure of retail customer service representatives using 129 biodata and assessment items. *SD* = standard deviation.

theaters, and other businesses. This service provider processed over 2.6 million employment applications in 2000, 7 million in 2002, and over 14.6 million in 2005. Approximately half of all incoming applicant data processed in 2004 were collected via the Internet.

As applicants are hired, hiring managers update new-hire records on-line, and the information is used to populate hiring documentation and employee records in the database. As employees terminate, the database is updated again via payroll data feeds and online exit surveys completed by managers and departing employees.

This last transaction creates a closed-loop employee record containing a standardized summary of the complete employment record of each person hired through the system. As of August 2004, over 1.7 million employee records had accumulated in the company's data warehouse, including 650,000 closed-loop records of former employees. This data environment creates opportunities for employee selection research using data from the thousands of employee records that flow through these companies every year. One example of this research was the development of an ESN trained to estimate length of service of customer service representatives for a national retailer.

An ESN was trained to estimate employee tenure (number of days on payroll) using data originally collected for other purposes. The predictor data were collected using a kiosk-based electronic employment application patterned after the client company's paper employment application form. A brief assessment of personality designed to assess customer service orientation followed completion of the application. The tenure criterion was obtained from payroll records by simply subtracting date of hire from date of termination to determine number of days on payroll. This neural validation project differs from the previous example in the following ways:

1. It was a pure data-mining application making use of data originally collected for purposes other than tenure model validation.
2. It resulted in the development of an ESN showing lower but usable validity coefficients and generalization.
3. It was deployed for a large national service company and is used to inform hiring decisions in a conventional test score reporting format embedded in a hiring report.

This ESN is shown in Figure 7.6 and is a backpropagation network with architecture 129:87:1. Predictor content consists of 80 unscaled biographic variables, the majority of which were nominal variables. Forty-nine of the inputs came from a 100-item assessment of customer service orientation. The network was trained on 30,000 cases, tested on 1,000 cases, and further tested for generalization on a holdout sample of 1,000 cases. The network was trained in 120,000 epochs using backpropagation learning for the hidden layer and conjugate gradient descent for the output layer. The unadjusted validity coefficients reported in Figure 7.6 are much lower than those reported in the previous example but were considered adequate for deployment to address very high turnover among customer service representatives at this firm.

Prior to the tenure ESN deployment, average tenure in the customer service population at this national retailer was 89 days, with annual turnover that exceeded 220%. An early prototype model (not shown) was implemented for approximately 10 months during which time average tenure for employees selected with the tenure model increased to 112 days and then began to decline. The research team discovered that several input variables used by the first network had been altered at the client's request, resulting in predictive model performance decline.

This second ESN was developed using a much larger validation sample than that of the previous model. One year later, average tenure among employees selected with either model had increased to 146 days. The absence of a randomized control group in this applied validation project prohibits

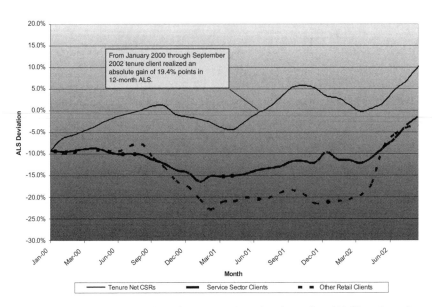

Figure 7.7. Longitudinal plot of average length of service (ALS) gains observed following tenure employee selection network deployment relative to other service and retail companies. CSRs = customer service representatives.

strong causal inferences to be made regarding validation model deployment and the observed increase in average length of service (ALS). However, tenure model client ALS was compared with other service sector and retail client ALS figures during the same period, with encouraging results shown in Figure 7.7 (Short & Yerex, 2002). Forthcoming research using randomized control group comparisons is in process at the time of this writing and is intended to provide a more conclusive evaluation of ESN deployment effects on ALS and other metrics.

Neural network validation research remains at an early stage. Widespread adoption of this procedure is unlikely without further research on the advantages, disadvantages, and appropriate use of neural validation methods. We anticipate that the number of early adopters of ESNs and academic research with these methods will accelerate as Internet-based hiring systems become commonplace. The new data environment created by these systems fundamentally changes the economics and scale of validation research.

ESNs and Equal Employment Opportunity

Computer-based employee selection procedures are potentially a great step forward for fair employment practices. Such systems are not subject to the selective perceptions, conscious and unconscious prejudices, and variable attention to task that characterize human interviewing and decision making. Networked computers and well-crafted user-interface tools bring consistency to the applicant experience and will apply the same standards of evaluation to every applicant. Computers cannot deviate from their programming, so disparate treatment cannot occur during the computer-administered portions of the hiring process. Even if hiring managers introduce illegal bias into the process, monitoring of compliance and adverse impact has the potential to identify potential problems. In addition, neural validity models can be evaluated for differential prediction and selection rate equivalence just as with conventionally scored assessments.

Selection fairness and lack of adverse impact is not guaranteed with any employment screening procedure. Empirical models of criterion validity, including neural networks, will model tainted performance criteria as easily as legitimate performance differences. Close attention and analysis of criterion measures for fairness can prevent perpetuation of past discrimination embedded in performance data. For example, if protected groups show significantly higher rates of involuntary termination compared to majority employees, a neural validation model of involuntary termination risk could show adverse impact. A thorough analysis of criterion fairness is time well spent and essential to deployment of selection models that meet both the letter and spirit of equal employment regulations.

In chapter 5 many studies comparing neural network and statistical methods were described and a body of evidence was presented suggesting functional equivalence of neural network and traditional statistical modeling. The major difference between the two approaches is that traditional statistical modeling begins from theory-based assumptions about how measured individual differences relate to measured differences in job performance. By empirically testing each hypothesized relationship, a formal model consisting of confirmed associations can be used to predict the future work behaviors of people who are yet to be hired. This approach has been used successfully for decades.

Neural network validation also begins with, but does not require, theory-based predictor content. Neural models may generalize better than conventional models when applied to the selection of future workers. However, neural modeling does not require that one anticipates all of the possible predictive associations resident in validation data. Nor does the neural approach require assumptions of orthogonal predictors, normal distributions, and linear association that characterize the majority of validation models in use today. In short, the neural network approach extracts useful predictive associations in sample data whether anticipated by scientist researchers or not.

If our behavioral theories are correct and operationalized effectively in validation research, these predictive associations will be assimilated and used by neural models. Conversely, if our behavioral theories are wrong, incomplete, or operationalized poorly, the upper limit of hypotheses-bound formal model accuracy is constrained. To be fair, neural model accuracy is also constrained by poor measurement; however, pattern recognition models are not restricted to theoretically anticipated associations and will make use of all detectable predictive relationships, including synergistic interaction effects, moderators, suppressors, and other complexities that tend to be neglected or ignored in human-configured modeling.

Pattern recognition algorithms have the potential to illuminate and refine theory as we uncover new and unexpected relationships in validation research. Neural validation methods, although still emerging, show promise for improving validation model accuracy and are particularly well suited for use in computer-based assessment and hiring decision support systems. Finally, neural modeling techniques present an efficient method for representing and using complexity observed in validation data that are easily missed with traditional human-specified predictive modeling.

8

USING SELF-ORGANIZING
MAPS TO STUDY
ORGANIZATIONAL COMMITMENT

Many problems in organizational research involve grouping related items into distinct and meaningful clusters. Clustering is based on reducing n-dimensional space to a smaller number of meaningful groups, and research can be either exploratory or confirmatory. A wide array of statistical methods is currently available to address clustering problems such as exploratory and confirmatory factor analysis, hierarchical clustering techniques, and k-means clustering. As might be expected, they are well represented in research in organizational psychology and organizational behavior.

Although these analytical methods have served researchers well, self-organizing maps (SOMs) have the potential to go beyond findings generated by conventional multivariate statistical methods. Indeed, their ability to extract patterns in data that are not easily uncovered by more conventional statistical methods is well documented (see Kiang & Kumar, 2001). This greater sensitivity can lead to *hidden* clusters (those embedded in groupings produced by conventional statistics) that might be of some value in either applied problem solving or theory building. Thus, the value of SOMs in organizational research lies in their ability to uncover patterns in data that might be masked by more conventional analyses.

As is the case with other clustering techniques, the purpose of the research can be purely exploratory so that it examines whether there are meaningful groupings in data. In this case, the researcher is simply attempting to determine if there are patterns in the data that might be of some value either in solving an applied problem or in theory building. It is also possible to use SOMs in a more confirmatory mode to examine whether certain patterns and profiles predicted by theory are plausible.

In this chapter we apply SOMs to the study of patterns of organizational commitment. This study is exploratory; theory and prior research findings provide no basis for hypothesizing new patterns of commitment to organizations. Rather, we are using SOMs to explore whether there are new patterns of attachment to organizations that might have been masked by more conventional analyses.

UNCOVERING PATTERNS OF COMMITMENT WITH A SELF-ORGANIZING MAP

Research on the topic of work-related commitment has grown steadily during the past few decades. Early studies were focused on commitment to organizations (Porter, Steers, Mowday, & Boulian, 1974), and this research stream gradually led to a broader interest in the general notion of work-related commitment (i.e., commitment to the job, career, organization, work group, and supervisor).

This broadening of commitment foci also resulted in a rethinking of the nature of commitment to work organizations. The scope of organizational commitment, in turn, was expanded to include three distinct forms of commitment: affective commitment, continuance commitment, and normative commitment (Allen & Meyer, 1990). Affective commitment was defined in terms of an emotional attachment to an organization characterized by support for the organization and acceptance of organizational values (Mowday, Steers, & Porter, 1982). In contrast, continuance commitment is grounded in H. Becker's (1960) notion of sunk costs and refers to an employee's perceived investments in an organization (Meyer & Allen, 1984). Finally, normative commitment is defined as a perceived duty to support the organization (Wiener, 1982).

As this broader conceptual frame was incorporated into research on work-related commitment, the distinction between foci and bases of commitment became salient. Foci refer to the object of commitment, that is, what one is committed to. Bases of commitment, however, capture the underlying motivational dynamic behind a given object-specific attachment (T. Becker & Billings, 1996).

By using concepts derived from Kelman (1958), three bases of commitment have been proposed: compliance, identification, and internalization (Caldwell, Chatman, & O'Reilly, 1990). Compliance engenders commitment to specific foci on the basis of perceived rewards or avoidance of punishment. Therefore, it is instrumental in nature. Commitment based on identification results from satisfying relationships and a desire for inclusion. It is emotional in nature. Finally, internalization refers to commitment based on value congruence and is normative in nature.

A natural outgrowth of this multidimensional view of work-related commitment is an interest in commitment profiles. Commitment profiles refer to distinct patterns of work-related commitment that have tangible consequences in organizations (Allen & Meyer, 1990; T. Becker & Billings, 1996). Linking patterns of commitment to outcome variables, in turn, is useful in (a) organizational diagnosis and intervention efforts (Reichers, 1986), (b) identifying functional and dysfunctional employees (Allen & Meyer, 1990), and (c) providing a better understanding of the relationship between foci and bases of commitment.

Searching for distinct patterns of work-related commitment is necessarily an applied and exploratory process. Research and theory have not advanced to the point at which expected patterns can be specified in advance so that formal hypothesis testing is not appropriate. This type of research problem, thus, is ideally suited to cluster analysis.

Interest in commitment profiles can be viewed as an extension of research based on multiple foci or bases of commitment. Although empirically derived (T. Becker & Billings, 1996), the identification of unique patterns of commitment has the potential to increase our understanding of commitment processes by linking multiple bases and foci of commitment to outcome variables. As such, generalizable commitment profiles can be viewed as an integrative approach to studying commitment processes in organizations that augments and enhances the antecedents→ intervening variables→ outcome variables models that characterize much of commitment research.

The practical value of commitment profiles has also been recognized. As noted by several writers, distinct patterns of commitment are useful in organizational diagnosis and intervention and in identifying productive and nonproductive employees (Allen & Meyer, 1990; Reichers, 1986).

Given their apparent value and the calls for future research on this topic, it is reasonable to expect to find a growing literature on commitment profiles. This has not been the case. Indeed, more than 10 years after Allen and Meyer (1990) suggested the topic of commitment profiles as a new area for research, only a few published studies on the topic are available (e.g., T. Becker & Billings, 1996; Carson, Carson, Roe, Birkenmeier, & Phillips, 1999).

T. Becker and Billings (1996) took a comprehensive approach to studying commitment profiles by using four foci (the organization, top management, the work group, and the supervisor) and three bases of commitment (compliance, identification, and internalization). Outcome variables included overall satisfaction, overall prosocial behavior, intention to quit, local satisfaction, and local prosocial behavior. The distinction between local (the work group and the supervisor) and global (the organization and top management) is central to the study and to interpreting its findings.

Four distinct commitment profiles emerged: committed, globally committed, locally committed, and uncommitted. Results with respect to the committed and the uncommitted were as expected, with respondents who were committed to all of the four foci of commitment exhibiting the most positive behavior and attitudes. Conversely, those who were committed to none of the four foci exhibited the least positive behaviors and outcomes.

Perhaps the most interesting finding that emerged was that the globally committed had a weaker overall identification and pattern of support for the organization than did the locally committed. T. Becker and Billings (1996) attributed this finding to the amorphous nature of global foci of commitment and suggested that additional research on the globally committed is needed.

A somewhat different interpretation of this finding is that the anomaly in the nature of the attachment of the globally committed might be the result of nonlinearities in the data (and possibly in commitment processes) that emerge as counterintuitive findings when linear methods are used. These types of findings provide justification for going beyond the usual statistical "toolbox" and using a more sensitive, nonlinear clustering technique such as SOMs.

In contrast to empirically derived commitment profiles, Carson et al. (1999) used a priori profiles based on the intersection of affective organizational commitment and career commitment to study the consequences of four patterns of commitment: committed, organizationally committed, career committed, and uncommitted. Results indicated that organizational and career commitment did not compete in that committed employees had most positive work outcomes and the weakest intention to quit. As expected, uncommitted respondents were the least satisfied and had the strongest desire to leave their organizations.

It is interesting to note that when groups were formed a priori using median splits, potential anomalies related to global commitment foci did not emerge. This result provides additional indirect evidence for using SOMs to study commitment profiles because the method by which the commitment groups were formed might have constrained nonlinearities in the data set.

CLUSTERING TECHNIQUES FOR DERIVING COMMITMENT PROFILES

Given that theory and research have not advanced to the point at which distinct commitment profiles can be specified a priori, clustering techniques that generate empirically derived profiles of work-related commitment seem to be the most useful way to advance research on this topic. This is an ideal study for SOMs for two reasons. First, the research is at an exploratory stage, and SOMs can extract nonlinearities in the data set that can be incorporated into theory building. Second, there is some research using traditional clustering techniques that can serve as a comparison and context for interpreting results from the SOM.

Given that we have explained the issues in defining and training a SOM in chapter 5, we will not go into great detail here about the steps and technical issues involved in building the network architecture and training a SOM. We refer readers back to chapter 5 or to Deboeck and Kohonen's (1998) book if a refresher is necessary.

THE STUDY: RATIONALE AND VARIABLES

A study of commitment profiles necessarily involves the use of a multidimensional definition of work-related commitment. The scope and focus of any study on this topic, in turn, are determined by the nature of the foci of commitment included in the study as well as the antecedent and behavioral variables used to complete the commitment profiles. Prior studies have taken a very broad view of commitment in that they were based on a wide range of foci of commitment (T. Becker & Billings, 1996). This approach was valuable because it provided a clear contrast between global and local foci of commitment. The emergent profiles, in turn, indicate that commitment to global foci needs additional clarification and study.

Researchers interested in integrating neural computing paradigms into their work would be well advised to look for situations very much like the one described earlier. Recall in chapter 4 that we provided general guidelines and a rationale for using neural networks for theory development in organizational research. Before we move on to the specific application of SOMs to study commitment profiles, it is important to use this opportunity to tie these general guidelines to a concrete example.

If we look at the pattern of findings that has emerged, although admittedly sparse, it is apparent that there is a potential anomaly with respect to commitment to global foci. This anomaly might be the result of sampling error or measurement error, but it also might be the result of nonlinearities in the data set. We believe that sampling or measurement error is not as likely as nonlinearity because results with respect to local foci of commitment were as expected.

Turning to the study variables, work-related commitment is defined in terms of commitment to the organization. Organizational commitment is the only form of work-related commitment that is hypothesized to be multidimensional in nature (Allen & Meyer, 1990) such that affective, continuance, and normative commitment are viewed as meaningful and distinct types of attachment to an organization.

The remaining variables used to define commitment profiles fall into three groups. The first grouping of variables includes two motivational bases of commitment: identification and internalization. The second grouping comprises outcome variables, including turnover intentions, turnover, and absenteeism. Finally, the third grouping of variables represents the work-related attitudes job satisfaction, job involvement, role conflict, and role ambiguity, which serve as contextual variables. Organizational tenure was included as a demographic variable.

The primary objective of this research is to examine patterns or profiles of organizational commitment using multiple forms of the construct. The use of SOMs is central to the study because we have reason to suspect that nonlinearities are present in the data and that these nonlinear patterns are partially reflected in anomalous findings using conventional analyses.

OVERVIEW OF METHODOLOGY

Data were collected at a large medical center located in the northeastern United States with a questionnaire survey. Respondents included staff and head nurses. Questionnaires were completed during normal working hours and were distributed and collected on-site. The sample of 335 was 97% female with a mean age of 32.4 years and a mean organizational tenure of 70.1 months.

Attitudinal variables were measured with established scales. Specifically, affective, continuance, and normative commitment to the organization were measured with Allen and Meyer's (1990) 8-item scales. Identification was measured with a 3-item scale tapping personal importance to the organization. This notion of personal importance is similar to the desire for inclusion characteristic of identification (Buchanan, 1974). Internalization was measured with a 4-item scale tapping person–organization value congruence. Job satisfaction was measured with Quinn and Staines's (1979) 5-item, facet-free scale. Job involvement was measured with a 15-item scale developed and validated by Lefkowitz, Somers, and Weinberg (1984). Role conflict and role ambiguity (expressed as role clarity) were assessed with Rizzo, House, and Lirtzman's (1970) measures. Job withdrawal intentions (expressed as intent to remain) were measured with Bluedorn's (1982) scale.

Behavioral data were taken from employee personnel records. Turnover data were gathered from employee personnel records. The measurement window for turnover was 12 months. All instances of turnover were voluntary. Two measures of absenteeism were used: total and annexed absences.

Total absences refer to the number of absences during a 12-month period. Annexed absences refer to the number of absences attached to weekend and holiday periods for the same 12-month period. Annexed absences are indicative of support for the organization because absences attached to holiday periods create staffing problems for crucial areas like care delivery.

DATA ANALYSIS: k-MEANS CLUSTERING AND SELF-ORGANIZING MAPS

Commitment profiles were formed using two clustering techniques: k-means clustering and SOMs. k-means clustering was chosen because it is the most similar to SOM among "traditional" clustering methods and because it generates nonoverlapping clusters. Differences among profiling variables across clusters were assessed with one-way analysis of variance using the Bonferroni correction for alpha inflation (Hays, 1988).

k-means clustering was performed using SPSS for the Macintosh. The Kohonen module of the Neural Networks package for Statistica for Windows was used to build and analyze the SOM. The number of nodes in the network and the choice of a two-dimensional output space are discretionary and were made by us. It should be noted that different choices (e.g., different network architectures) might have yielded different results. Furthermore, the decision as to when to terminate training of the Kohonen network on which the SOM is based is also discretionary and was made by us. Generally, training occurs in two stages. In the first stage, a very rough solution is produced with a small number (about 500) of epochs (i.e., passes of data through the network). Learning rates are then adjusted over a much larger number of epochs (10,000 or more) to refine the initial solution. This two-stage training procedure was used in this study.

FINDINGS: k-MEANS VERSUS SELF-ORGANIZING MAP

The k-means analysis generated a two-cluster solution. Clusters can be interpreted as "committed" and "uncommitted," and only with respect to continuance commitment. Furthermore, the majority of the sample (69%) fell into the uncommitted group. Comparison among the profiling variables across the two clusters was conducted with a one-way analysis of variance using the Bonferroni correction for alpha inflation (Hays, 1988). Statistically significant differences between the two clusters were noted for the following profiling variables: continuance commitment, organizational tenure, turnover intentions, and turnover rate. These findings are summarized in Table 8.1.

TABLE 8.1
k-Means Cluster Analysis With ANOVA Test Between Means

Profiling variable	Cluster 1 uncommitted $n = 264$	Cluster 2 committed $n = 78$	F
Tenure (months)	37.05	167	891**
Role conflict	3.78	3.39	6.45
Role ambiguity	4.1	3.83	4.13
Continuance commitment	2.81	3.10	13.49*
Affective commitment	2.73	2.92	5.58
Normative commitment	2.69	2.91	10.12
Job involvement	2.89	2.97	1.45
Job satisfaction	3.31	3.51	1.97
Personal importance	3.14	3.41	4.32
Value congruence	2.88	3.08	3.80
Intent to remain	4.91	5.58	14.01*
Absences	4.14	3.63	2.72
Annexed absences	1.75	1.43	.10
Turnover	.22	.03	10.29*

Note. $N = 348$. $*p < .05$. $**p < .01$.

In contrast, we extracted a four-cluster solution using a SOM based on a 7 by 7 network architecture resulting in 49 nodes. We assigned cases to these 49 nodes which we regrouped into four clusters: committed stayers, moderately committed stayers, committed leavers, and the uncommitted. Because we didn't assign all nodes on the map to a cluster, we only assigned 287 of the 348 cases to one of the four clusters.

We conducted a second one-way analysis of variance using the Bonferroni correction across these four clusters. Because there were more than two groups in this analysis, we conducted post hoc comparisons using the Scheffe method. Overall findings are summarized in Table 8.2.

It is noteworthy that results from the SOM are far richer than those from the k-means analysis. Eleven profiling variables emerged as statistically significant, representing a wide cross-section of the variables in the analysis, and included role conflict; affective and normative commitment; job involvement and job satisfaction; personal importance in the organization and person–organization value congruence; turnover intentions; absences; annexed absences; and turnover rate.

IMPLICATIONS

Although the notion of commitment profiles has intuitive appeal and practical implications, hardly any empirical research has been conducted on this topic. The few studies that are available suggest that a better under-

TABLE 8.2
SOM Analysis With ANOVA Test Between Means

Profiling variable	Cluster 1 committed stayers $n = 79$	Cluster 2 moderately committed stayers $n = 67$	Cluster 3 uncommitted $n = 114$	Cluster 4 committed leavers $n = 27$	F
Tenure (months)	92.43	70.94	60.08	70.00	3.67
Role conflict	3.51	3.07	4.38[a]	3.40	21.75**
Role ambiguity	5.09	5.36	4.56	5.49	12.88
Continuance commitment	3.09	2.76	2.82	2.75	4.13
Affective commitment	3.36	2.82[a]	2.25[a]	3.17	87.7**
Normative commitment	3.28	2.63[b]	2.37[a]	3.05	74.72**
Job involvement	3.26	2.82	2.69[a]	3.10	18.72*
Job satisfaction	4.05[d]	3.71	2.55[a]	3.48	40.12**
Personal importance	3.62	3.42	2.69	3.71	17.67*
Value congruence	3.46	3.01[a]	2.27[a]	3.62	28.12**
Intent to remain	5.95	5.36	4.03[a]	5.75	67.37**
Absences	3.38	5.64[a]	3.89	3.52	13.67*
Annexed absences	1.20	2.42[c]	1.90	1.76	18.16**
Turnover rate	.00	.00	.38[a]	.67[a]	43.89**

Note. N = 287. *p < 05. **p < .01.
[a]Differs from all other clusters. [b]Differs from clusters 1 and 4. [c]Differs from cluster 1. [d]Differs from clusters 3 and 4.

standing of commitment to global foci is needed to capture and validate distinct patterns or profiles of commitment (T. Becker & Billings, 1996). This study, in turn, was focused on profiles of commitment based on three forms of organizational commitment, an area of research suggested over a decade ago (Allen & Meyer, 1990).

The use of SOMs turned out to be crucial to the study because it was the only clustering method that yielded meaningful results. Specifically, k-means clustering identified two patterns of commitment, committed and uncommitted employees, that differed only in terms of continuance commitment, organizational tenure, intent to remain, and turnover. Thus, when one looks at these profiles in terms of the profiling variables, very little progress toward the general objective of identifying beneficial and detrimental patterns of organization is evident. Given that continuance commitment reflects tenure-based investments in the organization (Meyer & Allen, 1984), a case can be made that only two profiling variables distinguished these clusters or patterns of commitment; that is, high-tenure employees remained because the cost of leaving was too high.

Findings from the SOM were, however, markedly different. Four distinct profiles of commitment emerged that were labeled as follows: committed stayers, moderately committed stayers, committed leavers, and the uncommitted. Results also differed from k-means clustering in that the k-means analysis indicated that the majority of the sample was uncommitted (77%), whereas the SOM indicated that 60% of the sample was at least moderately committed to the organization. Furthermore, neither tenure nor continuance commitment emerged as a profiling variable in the SOM analysis.

These are important differences that suggest that traditional analyses are masking underlying dynamics in commitment processes and in patterns of commitment to organizations. From a statistical perspective, the SOM is most likely capturing and mapping nonlinear dependencies among affective and normative commitment in relation to the profiling variables.

These nonlinear dependencies, in turn, translate into four patterns of commitment that go beyond the traditional "committed–uncommitted" dichotomy. In particular, committed stayers exhibit a profile that is based on comparatively high levels of affective and normative commitment. Bases of commitment were consistent with these two foci in that committed stayers had the highest levels of person–organizational value congruence and felt that they were important members of the organization. Consequently, it is not surprising that committed stayers had the most positive work attitudes and that the turnover rate for this group was nil, which is consistent with a strong intention to remain with the organization. They also had the lowest incidence of total and annexed absences, the latter indicative of support for the organization. All told, this can be categorized as a beneficial pattern of commitment that is consistent with theory and prior research findings.

The profile for moderately committed stayers seems to provide some evidence that commitment can have negative, unintended consequences for organizations (Randall, 1987). Moderately committed stayers have formed comparatively strong bonds to the organization that are both affective and normative in nature. Like committed stayers, they are also satisfied with their jobs and have a strong intention to remain that resulted in no incidences of voluntary turnover. However, moderately committed stayers had a high incidence of absenteeism and a higher incidence of annexed absences than did uncommitted employees. These findings can be interpreted as indicative of a sense of entitlement suggesting that at moderate levels, commitment might be reflected in a desire for a comfortable work life. Although speculative, this appears to be an interesting line of inquiry for future research that would not arise from conventional analyses.

As might be expected, uncommitted employees felt alienated from the organization and had the lowest level of acceptance of organizational values. This sense of not belonging was reflected in negative work attitudes and the strongest intention to leave the organization. Turnover was evident in this group, with nearly 40% leaving voluntarily within 1 year. Somewhat surprisingly, despite low levels of commitment and job satisfaction, uncommitted employees did not have the highest levels of absences or annexed absences, suggesting that there was not a progression of withdrawal culminating in turnover. It is likely, however, that the overall negative pattern embedded in this profile did engender behaviors that were detrimental to the organization (e.g., hostility, lack of commitment to organizational objectives) so that turnover was probably welcome from both the individual's and the organization's point of view.

Finally, committed leavers represent a group that has not received much attention in the commitment literature in that high levels of commitment have been associated with low turnover (Mowday et al., 1982). Despite high levels of affective and normative commitment coupled with a sense of importance in the organization and acceptance of organizational values, the turnover rate for this group was 67%. Given that these are employees whom most organizations would like to keep, some consideration of why high levels of turnover occurred seems relevant. Turnover does not appear driven by a strong desire to leave, as intention to remain was fairly strong for this group. It is unlikely that each employee was presented with an unsolicited job offer, thus some job search activity probably took place. Examination of work attitudes indicates that although strongly committed to the organization, these employees were not satisfied with their jobs. Perhaps these comparative low levels of job satisfaction and job involvement triggered job search (Kopelman, Rovenpor, & Millsap, 1992), which then led to turnover. Although organizational commitment and job satisfaction are highly correlated, there might be instances (i.e., patterns of commitment) in which employees are highly committed to their organizations and comparatively dissatisfied with their jobs. The dynamics and implications of this pattern also seem to be an interesting area for future study.

This chapter demonstrated that, when used as an exploratory technique, SOMs can open up new insights and new ways of thinking about current research streams. In particular, had the data been analyzed solely with a conventional clustering technique, the research would not have offered any new insights into commitment profiles in work organizations. In fact, if this research had relied solely on traditional clustering methods such as k-means, it would almost certainly not pass muster in the peer review process, because no discernible contribution is evident. More to the point, we did not find anything of any value.

Research in finance and marketing using SOMs suggests that our findings are not atypical (Deboeck & Kohonen, 1998). Thus, mapping nonlinear dependencies among groups of related and well-chosen variables in organizational research might provide insights into long-standing problems that conventional analyses may have masked.

Both scholars and practitioners alike are bound to wonder if SOMs will produce similar results for them. The answer lies in a theme that runs through this book. If there are anomalies in current research that suggest the presence of nonlinearity, then SOMs are likely to produce results where hidden clusters are present. If, however, results are consistently weak across all profiling variables, it is more likely that no relationships among them are present (linear or nonlinear), and SOMs are not likely to offer new avenues to explore.

Researchers, therefore, would do well to look first at existing theory and research findings and then at SOMs as a possible solution if so indicated. Reversing this order will likely lead to disappointment and unjustified criticisms of SOMs.

III

IMPLICATIONS

9

LIMITATIONS AND MYTHS

Although neural networks have the potential to open up new avenues of research and to provide new insights into long-standing problems in organizational research, the neural computing paradigms that define artificial neural networks (ANNs) are not without problems. The purpose of this chapter is to address the limitations of neural networks to help researchers avoid obvious pitfalls and to offer a balanced treatment of the potential contribution of neural computing to organizational psychology.

One theme that runs through this book is that neural networks are different; that is, different from the analytical tools that the majority of academics and practitioners working in the field of organizational psychology and organizational behavior are familiar with, and different in significant ways. Consequently, they present different limitations and areas for caution than do conventional statistics. As such, the signposts that researchers commonly use to identify problems with conventional statistical analyses will not translate to neural computing. We begin the chapter with a discussion of the limitations of neural networks and then turn to myths associated with them.

LIMITATIONS OF NEURAL NETWORKS

Much of the controversy surrounding the use of neural networks stems from misconceptions about the capabilities and the limitations of neural networks. In this section, we discuss the limitations of ANNs and offer guidance in addressing them.

Training

Perhaps the most daunting element of using any neural computing paradigm is that there is no clear signal when the analysis is completed. Recall that data are passed through neural network architecture many times as patterns from input variables are mapped to output variables. Successive iterations generally lead to better solutions, but there is no clear stopping point. Rather, the number of training cycles is left to the researcher's judgment and experience.

If we contrast this situation with conventional statistical analyses, it is clearly unique. For example, a regression analysis is completed when a least squares fit is achieved. This is, of course, done with one pass of the data rather than the 100,000 or more that might be required to train a neural network.

As the fitting algorithms embedded in the hidden layer of a neural network are not geared to find a specific pattern in data (e.g., a least squares fit), the solution is not predetermined in that any pattern might emerge. This indeterminacy requires a multistage training and testing process to provide assurance that training has uncovered real relationships in the data set (see Garson, 1998; Haykin, 1994).

This is not a trivial issue because the number of training cycles used will have a significant effect on the results produced by the ANN. Too little training will not allow enough cases to pass through the network to accurately model patterns in the data, leading to incomplete and misleading results. Conversely, overtraining can lead to excellent predictions on the training data that do not generalize to the population; that is, the additional training has resulted in the modeling of sample-specific error (Ripley, 1996).

The idea of the same neural network architecture and the same data set producing different results depending on how training is managed requires a different approach to analysis. This characteristic of ANNs has been subject to criticism, with neural networks being cast as black boxes with limited learning capabilities (Asin, 2000; Olcay, 1999). We think it is best to be up front about this issue and present it as a limitation of neural networks.

For those readers who reach the conclusion that this limitation is severe enough to greatly limit the value of neural networks in organizational research, we offer the following arguments. First, although there is some degree of indeterminacy in training neural networks, there are metrics to assess the effectiveness of training as well. For example, with respect to overtraining, large discrepancies in predictions between training and test data are a clear indication that the network was overtrained (NeuralWare, Inc., 1994). When faced with this prospect, the network can be retrained to produce more generalizable findings. Second, there are statistical analyses with some degree of indeterminacy that have been very useful in organizational psychology research. Exploratory factor analysis is the most obvious in that determining the "correct" number of factors is an iterative process that has an intuitive component (Kim, 1978). One can think of the various analyses that must be conducted before a final factor structure is selected as a crude form of training, and one would be hard pressed to argue that factor analysis has not been a valuable tool in organizational research.

Network Architectures

Recall from chapter 3 that neural networks can be defined in terms of a distinct architecture with processing elements in the input, hidden, and output layers. The number of processing elements in the input layer is determined by the number of predictor variables, whereas the number of elements in the output layer is determined by the criterion variables (the exception being self-organizing maps, which are unsupervised).

As is the case with training, the characteristics of the hidden layer are determined by the researcher. That is, there are no hard-and-fast rules about the number of processing elements (or neurons) that compose the hidden layer, although guidelines are available (see Ripley, 1996). As is the case with training, different network architectures can produce different results with the same data (because mapping of inputs to outputs occurs in the hidden layer).

This indeterminacy might result in skepticism in that there is no clear and definitive network architecture for any given research problem. We view it as a characteristic of ANNs that is treated as a limitation that ought to be addressed in research studies. In other words, a rationale for choosing a given network architecture should be offered with some evidence that it produces better results than do competing architectures.

Preprocessing and Outliers

Preprocessing data are an important issue in training and using ANNs. Although there is evidence that ANNs handle deviations from normality among input variables better than do conventional statistics (NeuralWare, Inc., 1994), outliers can present serious problems in training and deploying neural networks (StatSoft, Inc., 2002).

To understand why this is so, it is helpful to briefly review the process through which neural networks uncover patterns in data. Recall that data are passed through the network many thousands of times and small adjustments are made to correct errors in prediction relative to known results. Because outliers are part of the data set, they are also passed through the network many thousands of times, and therefore can distort the solution produced by a neural network. That is, training might "settle" at a local minima or maxima and as a result incorporate outliers that lead to a distorted solution.

Thus, inspection and preprocessing of data are required *before* training is conducted. It is important to stress that the distributions of all variables to be included in the analysis must be examined, and careful attention must be paid to each variable. In some cases, outliers of little theoretical or practical interest can be eliminated. In others, variables can be transformed to smooth out distributions that are choppy or very badly skewed.

Interpretation

Interpretation of results from conventional statistical analyses is typically straightforward and can be defined in terms such as standardized regression weights or explained variance (Cohen & Cohen, 1983). Indeed, when we use a technique such as ordinary least squares (OLS) regression, there is little doubt which predictor variables were associated with the criterion variable. Nor is there any ambiguity about the relative contribution of the predictor variables.

The analog to regression weights in supervised neural networks is sensitivity analysis. Sensitivity analysis refers to the effect one variable in the model has on the criterion with other variables in the model held constant (StatSoft, Inc., 2002). Although there has been considerable progress in refining procedures for sensitivity analysis and this definition sounds very similar to that of a standardized regression weight, there is still work to be done before the equivalent of a beta weight emerges in the world of neural computing.

That having been said, the days of ANNs as black-box models that produce results that cannot be explained are also drawing to a close. Sensitivity analysis has evolved to the point at which graphical representations of high sensitivity areas (e.g., "hot spots") showing where the relative effect of two predictor variables interact on the criterion are increasingly common. They are usually expressed in three-dimensional space with two predictors and the criterion (Somers, 1999). Although work on sensitivity analysis represents an important breakthrough in neural computing, it is important to note that ease and thoroughness of interpretation of findings from ANNs lag behind that of conventional statistical models. We expect that advances in sensitivity analysis will close this gap over time.

MYTHS

Despite the growing popularity of neural networks in behavioral research, myths and misconceptions about them are still prevalent. It is important to understand what ANNs are and what they are not to use them effectively. We offer a discussion of some common myths to assist readers in evaluating and using neural networks in organizational research.

Myth 1: Neural Networks "Learn" in a Manner Similar to Human Learning

The biological analogy can be useful in understanding and conceptualizing neural network architectures and operations. However, when carried too far it can lead to a distortion of their properties and capabilities (Asin, 2000). Neural networks mirror the human nervous system in that they can be defined as a series of interconnected nodes with feedback loops. In particular, the processing elements in the hidden layer of a neural network develop threshold levels, and these elements are activated when the weights that they assign to improve prediction are changed. One may view this process of adjusting weights as a series of activation and deactivation cycles as the network finds patterns in data.

If using biological analogies such as activation thresholds helps readers understand how ANNs operate, then it is useful for those readers. However, it must be made clear that neural networks are not sentient, and they do not learn in the manner that humans assimilate and organize information. Rather, neural networks are statistical in nature and operate by using statistical functions to uncover patterns in data (Somers, 1999). To go beyond that statement serves to attribute properties to ANNs that they do not have, and in so doing, misrepresent what they are capable of doing.

In the future, advances in microprocessors will certainly lead to more powerful computing platforms for neural network application packages. In addition, developments in software engineering and in neural computing theory will likely lead to more efficient algorithms and more usable software. However, because neural networks are fundamentally statistical in nature, we do not believe that these advances mirror pattern recognition associated with human learning.

Myth 2: Neural Networks Will Always Outperform Conventional Statistical Models

Improvements in predictive accuracy that ANNs produce over conventional multivariate statistics and that are documented in this book can lead to the incorrect conclusion that ANNs *always* outperform conventional statistics. Although it is true that neural networks frequently produce better results when compared with more conventional statistical analysis, it is important to consider the conditions under which this occurs. ANNs are best suited to modeling the full range of relationships among variables and therefore are superior in uncovering nonlinear and complex interactions among variables. When such conditions are present in the data being analyzed, neural networks will outperform statistics derived from the general linear model because those statistical models cannot easily uncover patterns embedded in highly complex relationships among variables. However, when relationships among variables are primarily linear, neural networks offer no advantage over conventional statistical methods.

Myth 3: Neural Networks Can Be Trained to Produce Any Pattern of Results as Desired

It is a common misconception that ANNs can be manipulated to produce any pattern of results that a researcher desires or that neural networks can be trained to produce output that supports hypotheses or hunches. This is incorrect for two reasons. First, neural networks are pattern recognition algorithms that uncover patterns of relationships among variables. One of the unique and interesting features of ANNs is that they are able to capture relationships that are sometimes masked by other analysis (see Somers, 1999, 2001). However, if a pattern is not inherently present in the input data, no amount of training or "tweaking" of any neural computing paradigm will produce it. Researchers who believe otherwise will find themselves, much like Kierkegaard's (1992) blind man, looking in darkness for a black cat that is not there.

Second, although neural networks can capture patterns that are unique to a data set through overtraining, these "findings" have no scientific value. Although overtraining cannot produce specific results on demand, it can be used to conduct fishing expeditions when proper use of an ANN does not generate interesting or desired findings.

We do not view this as a serious problem because there are clear diagnostics that can be used to determine if a neural network has been overtrained. The most common is a significant decrement in performance on test data relative to training data (Garson, 1998). As such, an outside reader can easily determine if an ANN has been overtrained or request the information to make this determination. Our point here is that any statistical technique can be misused, and such misuse is not a weakness of the technique but rather of the researcher.

Myth 4: There Is No Relationship Between Neural Networks and Conventional Statistics

Because neural networks are most profitably viewed as statistical techniques rather than as biological process simulators, there are several ways that ANNs are related to conventional statistics. It is helpful to discuss them briefly to provide a better sense of how neural computing and conventional analyses can be used in concert to study the same phenomena.

To begin with, the same performance metrics can be used to assess results from neural networks and conventional analyses. With respect to continuous criterion variables, accuracy of prediction is expressed as the correlation between the predicted and observed values to determine R-squared and levels of explained variance. This metric can be computed for ANNs and more conventional analyses such as OLS regression. Similarly, percentage correctly classified serves as a common performance criterion for categorical variables for both ANNs and more conventional logistic regression techniques. Finally, for unsupervised or clustering problems, analysis of variance can be used to assess differences in profiling variables by cluster membership for conventional clustering techniques and for self-organizing maps.

Second, the patterns of interactions among variables that are uncovered by neural networks can be modeled by conventional statistics on a post hoc basis (Baatz, 1995). This task can be accomplished by using three-dimensional graphical relationships among variables produced by the neural network and then determining the appropriate interaction terms needed in regression analysis to reproduce the observed relationships. A high degree of correspondence between the results from the ANN and the results from regression analysis gives added confidence that the neural network has been trained and used properly. It also reinforces the point that neural networks uncover patterns in data that are not easily found using conventional statistics and that such patterns are real and reproducible.

Finally, both ANNs and conventional statistics assign weights to input variables to find patterns in data with respect to a known and measurable criterion. Although the process of assigning and modifying weights is more complicated in most neural computing paradigms, the underlying process is similar. As work in the area of sensitivity analysis continues, we believe that the process of how weights are determined will become clearer and, as that happens, ANNs will become more accessible to researchers.

Neural networks have certain limitations, and it is important that they be used with these limitations in mind. Failure to do so can lead to inaccurate prediction and poor model fit. Neural networks consistently perform better than linear models when sample data are nonlinear. They perform comparably with polynomial regression and other nonlinear modeling techniques when sample data show complex interactions among variables and extensive nonlinearity. Neural networks, as pattern recognition algorithms, have distinct advantages for exploring and identifying interactions and associations that can remain undetected using conventional modeling because of their ability to conduct an exhaustive search for these features. Finally, there is evidence indicating that neural networks tolerate faulty input data and may generalize pattern information to new data better than conventional models.

The disadvantages of neural network analysis provide some indication of when they may be inappropriate for a specific research application. Neural networks do not provide direct confirmation of specific hypotheses but must be interpreted on the basis of the characteristics of sample data and how they process individual cases. In applications that require fully specified models, a neural network may only be useful for assessing how much of the explainable variance is being captured by the specified model.

Myths have developed seemingly to explain neural networks' superior performance. In fact, neural networks are nothing more and nothing less than powerful pattern recognition tools. They do not learn as humans learn, they are not sentient, and they cannot be manipulated to produce desired results. What ANNs can do is to find and simulate patterns in data that could be missed with conventional statistical methods.

10

TRENDS AND
FUTURE DIRECTIONS

As artificial neural networks (ANNs) become more widely accepted in organizational research, they have the potential to influence how research questions are framed, how theory is developed, and how research findings are interpreted and applied. At present, interest in neural networks is comparatively low among social scientists, but there is a noticeable curiosity about ANNs among a small but growing group of scientists conducting both theoretical and applied organizational research (Aggarwal, Travers, & Scott-Conner, 2000; Chambless & Scarborough, 2002; J. M. Collins & Clark, 1993; Detienne, Detienne, & Joshie, 2003; Detienne, Lewis, & Detienne, 2003; Dickieson & Wilkins, 1992; Marshall & English, 2000; Ostberg, 2005; Palocsay & White, 2004; Sands & Wilkins, 1992; Scarborough, 1995; Scarborough & Somers, 2002; Somers, 1999, 2001; Stanton, Sederburg, & Smith, 2000; Thissen-Roe, 2005).

This chapter is intended to provide some notion of how ANNs might influence theoretical and applied behavioral research in organizations. We begin with a discussion of how neural networks are likely to affect the research process. Then we identify several areas in which more research is needed on neural networks applied to behavioral data in organizations. Finally, we suggest potential applications of neural modeling beyond those described in this book.

NEURAL NETWORKS AND BEHAVIORAL RESEARCH
IN ORGANIZATIONS

We believe that using neural networks changes the manner in which researchers approach any given problem or topic area. The typical adoption pattern for incorporating neural networks in a researcher's analytic toolbox begins with studying ANNs themselves. Given the comparatively steep learning curve, researchers typically spend considerable effort on "example" data and on learning the nuances of training a neural network.

Most ANN software packages include tutorials that make use of public domain sample data chosen to illustrate the capabilities of the software. Such tutorials begin with preprocessing the data and move through training and prediction exercises leading to results that are already well understood. These data sets are useful in learning how to train neural networks and explore the effects of different neural network architectures with respect to their performance (predictive accuracy). We suggest that the next step in becoming proficient with ANNs is to reanalyze data from one's own or published papers based on more conventional analyses using a neural network. Working in a domain area in which the researcher is familiar should be very helpful in developing a deeper understanding of the capabilities and limitations of neural networks.

Learning to use neural networks as an analytical tool can subtly change the way one approaches a specific research question. Interpreting the findings from an ANN is likely to take researchers into areas that are somewhat unfamiliar. This is especially the case when nonlinearity is present because it must be interpreted; that is, as complex relationships among variables are uncovered, they must be explained. The ensuing search for understanding is likely to be a driver of change in the field that will be reflected in the following trends.

Trend 1: Increased Integration of Quantitative and Qualitative Research

One of the most divisive and difficult debates in organizational psychology and organizational behavior is centered on the relative value of quantitative and qualitative research methodologies. Although there have been calls for "triangulation" and better integration of quantitative and qualitative methodologies in organizational research (see Jick, 1979), this has been slow to emerge. Indeed, it is reasonable to conclude that there are two factions, qualitative and quantitative researchers, who work more or less independently of each other and may not be aware of or value research done by the other.

Qualitative and quantitative research are based on established and highly specialized methodologies that have little in common other than an emphasis on empiricism. The research process is structured such that when either technique produces anomalous or provocative results, the common response is to conduct additional research using the same methodology. Thus, quantitative researchers conduct highly sophisticated post hoc analyses (often only to increase explained variance by 1% or 2%), whereas qualitative researchers seek additional field data or seek new insights in the data that they have collected.

Neural network procedures are more productive if the analyst makes an effort to become very familiar with sample data. This process begins in data preprocessing and moves through the training and validation phases of a neural network analysis. Researchers are required to be actively involved in the data analysis process and must often stop the network at various points in training to examine relationships among variables mapped by the network. Put simply, they have to be engaged in network training by guiding the mapping of the input variables to the outcomes. This process differs quite a bit from examining the output from a conventional statistical analysis, circling all of the statistically significant relationships, and then hoping that they are in the predicted direction.

Neural networks, therefore, require quantitative researchers to think more like their qualitatively oriented colleagues. Training an ANN involves uncovering relationships in data in a manner that is not dissimilar to developing grounded theory (Glaser & Strauss, 1967). That is, a researcher observes the behavior of a system through relationships among variables and then, on the basis of prior knowledge and theory, comes to some conclusion about what makes sense and what does not.

A connection to qualitative research can also be found in the interpretation of the results from an ANN. Suppose a researcher uses a neural network for the first time after months of learning and that a solution emerges in which relationships among input and outcome variables as demonstrated by wire-frame graphs show strong nonlinearity. The researcher is likely to be delighted until it comes time to interpret these results. Nonlinearity presents the challenge of explaining (in a meaningful way) why certain inflection points are present, that is, where small changes in the input variables lead to large changes in the criterion. Not only must the researcher explain why an inflection point has emerged (why there is nonlinearity), but he or she must also provide an explanation as to why it occurred at the specified ranges of the variables involved in the nonlinear pattern (Somers, 1999).

A classically trained quantitative researcher will almost certainly turn to results from prior quantitative studies for guidance in interpretation.

Because virtually all of this research is likely to be based on linear models and linear methods, it will often be of little value in interpreting nonlinear findings. After some thought, it will become apparent that the secret of interpretation lies in a better understanding of the processes underlying the nonlinear dynamics.

It is at this point that qualitative studies on the topic of interest and in related areas become relevant because they are useful in understanding why inflection points occur and why they might occur at specified ranges of certain variables. For example, Somers (1999) used neural networks to model turnover and found that there are clear areas of high sensitivity in which small changes in predictor variables lead to a greatly increased probability of turnover. T. W. Lee and Mitchell's (1994) application of image theory to the turnover process was very useful in understanding this result, especially when it was augmented with qualitative studies of the psychodynamics underlying the decision to leave. Furthermore, it is noteworthy that traditional turnover theory and research was not useful in interpreting Somers's (1999) findings.

We believe that as ANNs begin to uncover nonlinear relationships and, in the process, raise more questions than they answer, researchers will be challenged to look to less familiar research findings and more to new conceptual frameworks that lie outside the immediate domain under study. This search is often driven by the desire and need for a greater understanding of process. Valuable new insights are likely to be found in qualitative studies; for that reason, we believe that greater adoption of ANNs will lead to a greater reliance and a greater acceptance of qualitative research methodologies in organizational psychology.

Trend 2: More Exploratory Studies Focused on Vexing Problems

The "model" study in the behavioral sciences in general and organizational psychology in particular is based on formal hypotheses grounded in theory. As such, the variables that are included and the nature of the relationships among them are predetermined, and the study is evaluated on the extent to which the hypotheses were supported.

Although there is nothing to argue with here per se, if relationships among the variables are primarily linear and the level of explained variance or the overall robustness of the findings is sufficient, there is little incentive for researchers to use neural networks for this type of study. Indeed, the computational overhead, added complexity, and relatively steep learning curve are likely to result in frustration as results from ANNs will be no better than those produced by conventional multivariate statistics.

Researchers interested in learning to use neural networks are likely to do so to gain insights into topic areas in which progress using conventional methods falls short of expectations. More specifically, the topic areas that are investigated with neural networks are most likely to be those with a history of disappointing results and the general sense that there ought to be stronger relationships among predictor and criterion variables than those generated by previous empirical research.

Given that these topic areas are problematic by definition, it is not possible or appropriate to specify the nature of relationships between antecedent and outcome variables in advance. For example, in discussion of support for a relationship between job satisfaction and job performance, Guion (1992a) suggested using curve fitting to observe if, where, and how these two variables might be related. Although neural networks are considerably more powerful than curve fitting, the basic philosophy supporting their use in organizational psychology is not much different from the one proposed by Guion when he suggested that researchers get back to basics and start plotting relationships among variables.

Our point here is that in the domain areas and the specific research questions within organizational psychology and organizational behavior in which neural networks are likely to be most useful, it will not be possible to specify the nature or even the specific patterns of relationships among variables in advance. Consequently, research studies using ANNs will most likely be framed in terms of research questions rather than in terms of formal hypotheses.

Although some will surely see this as "dustbowl" empiricism, it is important to recognize two important reasons why this is not the case. First, ANNs are being used in areas in which traditional methods and well-established theories have either "hit a wall" or have not lived up to their promise. At this point, it is appropriate to explore new ways of looking at old problems. It is also appropriate to take a more exploratory approach because it is the start of a new research direction. Second, the purpose of this research ought to be to open new insights into old problems leading to modifications of theory with the intention of progressing to the point at which confirmatory studies can be conducted using ANNs and related techniques.

It is useful to examine how this process might work in practice. Somers (2001) was inspired by Guion's (1992a) proposition that the relationship between job satisfaction and job performance might be nonlinear as well as his call to use nontraditional methods to study the relationship between these two variables. The suggestion that job satisfaction has a nonlinear relationship to job performance represents a break from the past and is an interesting idea, but it is not a formal hypothesis.

A formal hypothesis must be more precise and state the specific form of the nonlinear relationship. Thus, Guion's (1992a) "hypothesis" was more of a proposition that posed the suggestion that potential nonlinearities in the relationship between job satisfaction and job performance ought to be examined. Confirmation of moderate or pervasive nonlinearity, in turn, suggests that we need to rethink the relationship between job satisfaction and job performance, whereas disconfirmation implies that these two variables are probably not related.

Somers (2001) used a Bayesian neural network to study the relationship between job satisfaction and job performance rather than a curve-fitting model. The study had no formal hypotheses but rather examined the proposition that the relationship between these two variables was, indeed, nonlinear. The study was truly exploratory in that it offered the possibility that there might be a nonlinear relationship between job satisfaction and job performance. (There was, in fact, no evidence that this is so, and there is no basis for positing such a relationship other than the failure of linear methods to produce expected results.) Furthermore, no attempt was made to specify the nature of the nonlinear relationship in advance. To do so would have been disingenuous at best and intellectually dishonest at worst because there was no basis in theory or in empirical research to even begin to guess about the form of any proposed nonlinear relationship.

The results from the Bayesian neural network indicated that there is a relationship between job performance and job satisfaction but that it is highly "channeled." That is, it occurs only within a small fraction of the range of job satisfaction so that there are large areas of low sensitivity in which there is, in fact, no relationship between job satisfaction and job performance. There are other more targeted ranges, however, in which the relationship is fairly strong.

We can use this study as an illustration of how ANNs are likely to affect research in organizational psychology. Their ability to increase explained variance by mapping nonlinear dynamics will lead researchers to explore more propositions or hunches, resulting in a greater percentage of exploratory studies in the field. We would like to make the point that although this approach can be a driver of innovation and new insights, it is imperative that findings from ANNs eventually be used to develop and test theory. That is, there should come a time when neural networks are used to test confirmatory hypotheses that were derived from theory generated by prior exploratory studies.

Trend 3: Toward Greater Examination of Microprocesses

Researchers in organizational behavior and organizational psychology are frequently faced with situations in which results fall far below expectations: That is, levels of explained variance are low even though theory suggests that antecedent variables or predictor variables should have a strong effect on the criterion. The most common approach to addressing this situation is to expand the number of variables in the theoretical model and often the number and complexity of the interactions among them as well.

For example, in addressing the failure to improve our understanding and ability to predict turnover, T. W. Lee and Mowday (1987) built a comprehensive model of turnover that greatly expanded the number of variables in the core turnover sequence and increased interactions among them as well. The end result of this added complexity was a minimal increment in explained variance in the criterion. In other words, additional variables did not lead to incremental variance.

Our intention is not to be critical of T. W. Lee and Mowday but rather to point out the basic approach to theory development and refinement when results are not as desired (which is often in our field). It is helpful to consider why researchers would take this approach, especially when it is almost always unsuccessful. We offer two reasons. The first stems from the prevailing view of science in organizational psychology and organizational behavior that we refer to as scientific realism (see Bunge, 1967). Science is, of course, based on parsimony so that it is appropriate and expected to develop theoretical models that are as simple as possible. As these models produce poor results through repeated empirical testing, it is also reasonable and appropriate to consider which key variables in the process might be missing. This exercise of testing and refinement, in turn, leads to bigger and more expansive models in an attempt to capture the richness of the phenomena under study. This general approach is, in and of itself, not problematic provided that the expanded models perform as expected. Indeed, one could argue that the research stream was moving toward defining the point at which the model was as complex as necessary.

The second reason comes from the methodology through which hypotheses are tested. The majority of research in organizational behavior and organizational psychology uses nonexperimental survey designs. Accordingly, the primary methodological technique is some derivative of multiple regression analysis. From a practical standpoint, the only ways to increase explained variance with a regression model are to reduce measurement error or to increase the number of variables in the model and the interactions among them. Progress in the measurement arena has been slow at best so that the primary option that researchers have to improve predictive accuracy is to build bigger, more complex models, and this is what they have done.

In contrast, neural networks model the full range of relationships among variables, including the multiple-way interactions that are often added to conceptual models to improve predictive accuracy. This powerful approach often produces results that are better than those generated by conventional statistics. As a result, the challenge that researchers face is not finding ways to improve predictive accuracy but rather attempting to understand why increments in explained variance were observed. This challenge does not involve adding new variables to the model. Instead, it is necessary to develop a compelling rationale as to why existing relationships were observed and what they might mean.

At this point, it is helpful to consider how results from an ANN can redirect a researcher's thinking. Suppose, for example, that a study using neural networks yields a sizable improvement in predictive accuracy relative to ordinary least squares regression. Academicians are expected to offer some explanation as to why this finding was observed if they wish to publish their research in high-quality scholarly journals. Similarly, practitioners will want to have some sense of the processes underlying their findings if they plan to use the results from an ANN to make business decisions.

We know that if an ANN outperforms conventional statistics, the underlying reason is moderate to pervasive nonlinearity and interactivity. Interpretation and understanding of the findings from an ANN, in turn, involve tackling the nonlinear relationships among variables that emerged. There are two tools that are very useful in accomplishing this objective. The first is wire-frame or three-dimensional surface graphs that map relationships among sets of predictor variables and the criterion (see chap. 3). The nonlinear patterns reflected in these graphs are critical to understanding the nonlinear dynamics uncovered by the neural network, and researchers should pay careful attention to them.

The second is sensitivity analysis (Ripley, 1996). Sensitivity analysis is an analog to the beta weights produced by regression analysis, and it captures effect of the change in predictor variable on the criterion variable with other variables in the model held constant. Sensitivity analysis forces the researcher to consider the ranges of the variables being studied because (if nonlinearity is present) changes in the level of predictor will not lead to uniform changes in the level of the criterion. The areas of high sensitivity identify where nonlinearity is present and suggest where researchers may want to direct their efforts to understand and interpret the underlying processes.

Interpreting the results from an ANN, therefore, directs researchers to think smaller rather than bigger. As a consequence, they are faced with developing a deeper understanding of relationships among variables being studied and then mapping that understanding back to theoretical processes. More specifically, they need to develop preliminary and then more convincing explanations about why the ranges of high sensitivity occur where they were observed. To do so involves clearer specification and modification of existing processes rather than the expansion of existing processes. As a result we would expect to see greater levels of adoption of neural networks in organizational research leading to more "microprocess"-type research.

Summary

These three trends are clearly interrelated and point to a potentially significant new direction for research in organizational psychology and related areas. We think it is important to consider the full implications of more widespread adoption of ANNs in organizational psychology because there is a commonly held view that neural networks are useful in improving predictive accuracy and that their influence will not go beyond that arena. We very much disagree. Although we would be hard pressed to think of neural networks as triggering a paradigm shift, they do have the potential to have more far-reaching effects on the field than simply producing better empirical results. These effects are likely to be subtle and incremental, but researchers should be aware of them.

OPPORTUNITIES FOR NEW RESEARCH

There are many opportunities for meaningful contributions to our understanding of using neural networks in organizational research. Compared with other statistical procedures, neural network modeling is a fairly new analytic capability for social scientists, and the literature on their use in this domain remains sparse. Furthermore, the literature describing neural network applications in organizational research has been (with some exceptions) devoted to describing and testing these methods rather than using neural modeling to conduct research. The research areas suggested are not intended to be exhaustive, and we hope that the inquisitive reader will begin to assess applications of neural network analysis within his or her area of research.

Research on Neural Network Interpretation

We have described three-dimensional surface graphs and sensitivity analysis as useful methods for interpreting a neural model. Other procedures have been discussed (Chryssolouris, Lee, & Ramsey, 1996; Garavaglia, 1993; Garson, 1991b; Schrodt, 1991), but it is safe to say that the utility of neural network analysis for behavioral research could be greatly improved with better methods for interpreting neural network models.

Research Testing Different Neural Network Paradigms Applied to Behavioral Data

Research describing the use of backpropagation, radial basis functions, general regression, and Kohonen self-organizing map neural network paradigms has only begun to establish the utility of neural modeling with behavioral data (see chap. 5). In the taxonomy of neural network paradigms presented in chapter 2, we identify 10 common types of supervised networks, and most of these have not been evaluated for use in organizational research applications. There is much to learn about the relative performance of different types of trained neural networks in our field and the conditions affecting neural network analysis utility. Some research in this has been reported (Depsey, Folchi, & Sands, 1995; Leslie & Hanges, 2005).

Research Combining ANN Procedures With Other Statistical Methods

As mentioned previously, we expect neural modeling techniques to have synergistic utility when combined with other sophisticated procedures, particularly those that are nonlinear. Thissen-Roe (2005) used item response theory to consolidate redundant inputs to a neural criterion validation model, allowing the use of more inputs per training case. By using a neural network to switch between measuring several personality dimensions in an adaptive test, this research addressed a problem that either technique alone could not solve.

Chambless and Scarborough (2002) applied information-theoretic methods to feature selection for neural modeling. The use of information-transfer values, an assumption-free metric, to identify second- and third-order interactions between input variables improved explainable variance in trained neural models over linear feature selection.

From other disciplines, similar lines of research are emerging. C. Lee, Rey, Mentele, and Garver (2005) described the development of a structured neural network model of customer loyalty and profitability using a combination of backpropagation neural networks and structural equation modeling. B. Collins (2000) used trained neural network models to generate randomly seeded constructed data sets of observed influence scale data (C. Lee & Marshall, 1998) to fit a structural equation model of family decision-making processes.

Organizational Research Using Neural Networks and Other Artificial Intelligence Techniques

In 1965, Lofti Zadeh coined the term *fuzzy set* and developed the membership function and operations that describe mathematically the extent to which something either is or is not something else (Zadeh, 1965). Fuzzy set theory allows mathematical (hence, computational) description of vagueness, which has found many applications in control theory. Discrete, dichotomous descriptions of absolutes (is vs. is not; black vs. white; yes vs. no; one vs. zero, etc.) describe a reality that does not exist. No person is completely introverted or completely extroverted, intelligent or unintelligent, experienced or inexperienced. The reality of individual differences is actually an interactive, temporally defined fuzzy phenomenon that changes under different measurement conditions.

Future research in applied psychology may use fuzzy variable definition and modeling techniques. Fuzzy models of psychological variables will allow mathematical description of overlapping state–trait phenomena with multidimensional gradient boundaries. Theoretically, fuzzy logic and neuro-fuzzy optimization would allow specified (explainable) models to be developed from feed-forward neural network training. Hybridization of ANNs' ability to learn from data has a natural synergy with the ability of fuzzy systems to quantify linguistic inputs and give a working approximation of complex system input–output rules (Haykin, 1999). For more information on fuzzy logic and neuro-fuzzy optimization, see Kosko (1992), Cox (1995), von Altrock (1996), or Wang (2001).

NEURAL NETWORK APPLICATIONS

Organizational research is an applied discipline, and neural networks are very practical and flexible modeling tools. Their ability to generalize pattern information to new data, tolerate noisy inputs, and produce reasonable estimates reliably has real value in an online world. One of the criticisms of this book from our insightful group of reviewers was about the small number of real-world applications of neural network modeling in organizational research. There are still only two detailed examples of neural network research in this book for a very simple reason: Very few ANN applications appear in the literature of organizational psychology.

We have described the use of neural networks for behavioral prediction in the context of employee selection and research on the use of self-organizing maps. Other than the literature we reviewed in chapter 6, behavioral research using neural modeling techniques is still fairly rare at the time of this writing. We expect this to change.

Extending the logic of pattern recognition analysis to behavioral research in organizations can take at least two paths. If the research problem involves prediction or estimation of a measurable behavior or outcome, scanning (or building) the data environment for antecedent or associative measures of theoretically linked phenomena allows training of a feed-forward neural network. Often, as is the case with employee selection, the research domain is already well understood, and the application of pattern recognition tools is a logical extension of previous research. Alternatively, if the linkage between independent and dependent variables is poorly understood or indeterminate, exploratory use of a trained neural network can be used to determine modeling feasibility and to estimate explainable variance with that set of input variables.

If the research goal is to improve understanding of behaviors or outcomes by grouping similar cases, identifying interactions, and reducing interpretive complexity, then a self-organizing map network may be useful. For example, self-report survey data can be used to train a self-organizing map to group cases of similar response patterns as described in chapter 8. We are confident that as these procedures are adopted for behavioral research and as graduate training programs incorporate neural modeling as a useful component of multivariate analysis, wider application of neural networks will occur. Reasoning down these two paths, we expect the following applied research domains to adopt or continue to experiment with neural nets.

Consumer online behavior: A vast amount of data is collected every day as millions of Internet users surf the Web. Making sense of the data created by online shoppers, interactive gamers, illegal hackers, virus launchers, Internet gamblers, survey respondents, spammers, and other populations of interest may be accessible to neural network modeling.

Employee online behavior: Many jobs require extensive use of computers and other online equipment such as point-of-sale systems. We are aware of one proprietary application of neural networks used to model pretheft consequence testing by cashiers in a large retailer. In this application, observed patterns of overage and underage, returns, refunds, and other transaction activity by individual cashiers are used to generate an exception report that triggers increased surveillance or warnings to the employee of increased surveillance to prevent theft (Scarborough, 2004). This application is very similar to the credit card activity monitoring networks mentioned earlier. Among professional employees with ready access to e-mail and the Internet, online behavior is likely to have systematic patterns related to productivity, voluntary turnover, delinquency, and other behaviors.

Succession planning, promotions, and placement: Most large employers maintain files of the qualifications and work experience of current staff. If employee records are in quantified form and matched to measures of promotions and management effectiveness, the elements for training a neural model to estimate management potential could be developed.

Human resource planning: Forecasting headcount and hiring activity on the basis of current trends and future requirements is an estimation problem that can be adapted for neural modeling. Inputs such as past operating volume and projected changes, seasonal and competitor effects, workforce demographics, year-over-year performance metrics, turnover trends, and other leading indicators are often available in historic data sets. If historic headcount is accepted as a criterion measure, training a network using historic data can provide estimates for future periods.

Jury selection: Attorneys often employ psychologists to evaluate attitudes and beliefs of potential jurors and assess the probability of siding for or against their case. The use of structured questionnaires about juror biographic facts, belief systems, attitudes, and traits to predict juror behavior is possible with a sufficient sample of juror attitudes and decision outcomes using mock trial data.

Neural networks are being used every day all over the world to model phenomena at the very edge of our scientific understanding. From mapping the human genome to modeling global warming, pattern recognition-based problem solving is an accepted analytic capability in the physical sciences. Often, neural network applications have been successfully deployed to solve practical problems by modeling phenomena that are too complex to model any other way. We believe that neural networks will find a similar niche in organizational science as well.

The environment in which modern organizations operate is likely to continue to evolve toward greater complexity. Our ability to measure populations and processes using computer networks and databases will continue to improve as well. Neural network procedures can apprehend, represent, and report on great complexity. As we come to understand the advantages and limitations of these procedures and master their use, we have the opportunity to participate in and contribute to a better understanding of the world we live in.

APPENDIX: BACKPROPAGATION ALGORITHM

Rumelhart, Hinton, and Williams (1986) described a backpropagation algorithm by which error in a network's output could be distributed among its network connection weights to adjust them. Prior to the work of Rumelhart et al., a rule had existed for adjusting the weights of a network with no hidden layers. Following the presentation of vector pattern p, the weight W_{ji} of the connection between input node i and output node j is adjusted according to

$$\Delta_p W_{ji} = \eta \varepsilon_{pj} X_{pi}, \tag{1}$$

where η is a scalar constant called a learning coefficient that determines the rate at which the connection weights are modified, X_{pi} is the value of the ith element of input pattern p, and $\Delta_p W_{ji}$ is the change made to the weight from the ith to the jth element. The error term ε_{pj} represents the difference between the desired output T_{pj} and the actual output X_{pj},

$$\varepsilon_{pj} = T_{pj} - X_{pj}. \tag{2}$$

As a gradient descent algorithm, the goal of training using the generalized delta rule is to minimize error by adjusting all Ws (connection weights). The quantity to be minimized is the average across patterns of the total error energy

$$E_p = \tfrac{1}{2} \Sigma \, \varepsilon_{pj}^2 \tag{3}$$

of all outputs.

Under the backpropagation algorithm, the adjustment to connection weight W_{ji}, which may no longer be a direct connection between an input and an output, is calculated as

$$\Delta W_{ji} = -\eta \; \delta E_p / \delta W_{ji}. \tag{4}$$

This allows for the "passing back" of error to weights in earlier layers because the effect of those weights on intermediate activations can be calculated.

Backpropagation requires the use of transfer functions $F_j(x)$ which are continuous and differentiable. $F_j(x)$ is the function relating the inputs to a node to its output X_{pj}:

$$X_{pj} = F_j(\Sigma X_{pi}), \tag{5}$$

where X_{pi} are the outputs of the previous layer.

Using the chain rule of calculus, we can compute $\delta Ep/\delta W_{ji}$ for the second-to-last layer according to

$$\delta E_p/\delta W_{ji} = -\varepsilon_{pj} \, F'j(\Sigma \, X_{pi}) \, X_{pi}. \tag{6}$$

The connection weights are then updated using

$$W_{ji}(\text{new}) = W_{ji}(\text{old}) + \Delta_p W_{ji}. \tag{7}$$

A common modification to the generalized delta rule includes the use of a scalar constant known as a momentum term (α).

$$W_{ji}(\text{new}) = W_{ji}(\text{old}) + \Delta_{pi} W_{ji} + \Delta_{p-1} W_{ji*} \alpha \tag{8}$$

The momentum term helps smooth the local curvature between successive squared error surfaces and in some cases will prevent convergence in a local minimum. Non-convex ridges in the energy surface are like gullies on the side of a hill. Local minima can trap the network in equilibrium at a point higher than the global minimum mean squared error. Further discussion of the backpropagation derivation can be found in Kosko (1992), Reed and Marks (1999), and Rumelhart et al. (1986).

GLOSSARY

Activation Function: A function within an artificial neuron that processes incoming values from other neurons and determines whether the incoming vector will result in an output value passed on to the next layer of neurons. A common activation function is a linear threshold giving outputs between 0 and 1. The state of activation of a neuron describes whether or not the incoming signal triggers output from the neuron to the next layer. The activation function, also called a transfer function, can be bounded or unbounded, discrete or continuous, linear or nonlinear depending on the neural network paradigm. In nonlinear networks, sigmoidal and hyperbolic tangent transfer functions are most common.

Axon: A structure that connects biological neurons to each other. Electrical impulses pass from the axon of the originating cell (outputs) through a synaptic junction to the dendrites of the next cell in the network that processes the signal as an input.

Backpropagation: A class of feed-forward neural networks used for classification, forecasting, and estimation. Backpropagation is the process by which connection weights between neurons are modified using a backward pass of error derivatives.

Biodata: Biographical facts or questionnaire responses related to life history, job experience, training programs, and other personal background information used in employee selection. Biodata variables are facets of applicant background that are quantified, ranked, or categorized for mathematical representation and processing.

Cascade Learning: A method for optimizing a feed-forward neural network's architecture for a specific modeling problem. In cascade learning, the number of neurons in the hidden layer is systematically increased during training. When additional neurons do not result in lower error, the last neuron(s) added is deleted and the remaining number of neurons is considered optimal.

Competitive Learning: A class of learning rules used by Kohonen networks and other self-organizing maps to cluster related cases and collapse dimensionality. Competitive learning can be either deterministic (the same neuron always maps the position of a specific case) or distributed (near-neighbor neurons approximate the centroids of related cases).

Computational Energy Surface: A graphic representation of the error surface traversed by a gradient-descent algorithm as input vectors are mapped to the objective function during neural network training (see also *global minima, local minima*).

Connection Weights: Parameters representing connections between neurons.

Convergence: In neural training, the point at which gradient descent slows or stops, indicating a stable connection weight matrix giving minimum error output. Convergence does not necessarily mean that the global minima has been reached (see *local minima*).

Delta Rule: A learning rule for updating the connection weight matrix in a trained feed-forward neural network. It uses least mean square (LMS) regression of the error term to recursively minimize the difference between neural net output and observed correct values.

Deterministic Model: A mathematical model or theory that deterministically predicts the specific value of a dependent variable or output given a set of independent variables or inputs.

Ensemble: An ensemble of neural networks is a group of networks trained on the same data set to estimate the same dependent variable. Agreement among models improves confidence in the overall estimate(s).

Epoch: In neural network training, a complete pass of all cases in a training sample through the network. Training to convergence can require hundreds of thousands of epochs for highly complex problems with many variables. Simpler problems require fewer training epochs.

Error Term: In feed-forward neural networks, the difference between the network estimate of the dependent variable and the actual dependent variable used to train (fit) the network.

Feed-Forward Network: A type of neural network that processes independent variables (case vectors) sequentially in one direction from an input layer of neurons, through one or more hidden layers to an output layer. Feed-forward networks, such as backpropation or regression networks, are trained to fit a set of input variables (also called predictor or independent variables) to a corresponding known criterion or independent variable.

Fuzzy Set: A group of fuzzy variables. Fuzzy or multivalued logic was formally described by Lotfi Zadeh (1965) as a means for expressing numeric values in multivalent terms. Fuzzy logic allows computational processing of verbal concepts expressing degrees of certainty, membership, valence, and contradiction.

Global Minima: The location in a multidimensional space of input vectors showing minimum error between network estimates of the dependent variable and the objective function (observed values). When the error term is graphically represented on the z-axis of a three-dimensional surface graph such that lower error values are near the origin, the global minimum is the lowest point on the error surface (see also *computational energy surface, local minima.*)

Gradient Descent Algorithm: One of many computational approaches to minimizing error between a model estimate and the actual values of a dependent variable (see also *backpropagation, delta rule, learning rule*).

Hidden Layer: In neural network architecture, a group of neurons that share the same sequential position in the overall architecture but are connected only to other neurons. Hidden-layer neurons receive the processed output of the previous layer of neurons and in turn pass their output to neurons in the next layer. In a statistical sense, the hidden layer is analogous to additional interaction terms in regression. Small hidden layers are more parsimonious but cannot represent high dimensionality and complex interactions as well as hidden layers with more neurons. Too many hidden neurons and the network will memorize the training data or learn spurious sample-specific noise. Heuristics for setting an initial number of hidden-layer neurons are discussed in chapter 5, but experimentation with different hidden-layer neuron counts is appropriate and necessary. In practice, neural networks requiring more than one hidden layer are rare.

Input: A single data point. Input is used to refer to the independent variable(s) in a data set or the individual values of the independent variable for a single case or record. Neural nets process inputs as vectors, with each individual value representing a position in one dimension.

Input Layer: The first group of neurons in a neural network architecture to receive and process input vectors. In trained feed-forward networks, each independent variable is given one input neuron so that in most network architectures, the number of input-layer neurons equals the number of input variables (see also *hidden layer, output layer*).

Layer: In neural network architecture, a group of neurons with the same sequential positioning in the overall network. Conventional notation of neural network architecture is given by sequential counts of neurons by layer. For example, a three-layer network with four input-layer neurons, three hidden-layer neurons, and one output neuron would be shown as 4:3:1 (see also *hidden layer, input layer, output layer*).

Learning Rule: The algorithm that specifies how connection weights are updated each time the network is given a new input vector to process.

Linear: A term describing the relationship between two variables X and Y where the value of Y changes by a constant amount relative to single unit changes in X. If the amount of change in Y varies as X increases or decreases by one, the relationship between X and Y would be described as *nonlinear*.

Local Minima: Locations on the energy (error) surface appearing as basins or valleys of localized reduced error that are higher than the global minima. Local minima represent suboptimal locations for network convergence. If training is discontinued, model performance will have higher error than if training continues to the global minima (see also *computational error surface, global minima, gradient descent*).

Neuron: A single processing element in a neural network. The most common form of neuron has two basic parts: a summation function that receives inputs and a transfer function that processes inputs and passes the processed values to the next layer of neurons. If the neuron is in the last layer of the network, the output is the final estimate of the dependent variable for that input vector or case.

Noise: As in "noisy data," a term used to describe the quality of research sample data. It is a conceptual term borrowed from signal processing, for which it is used to describe the amount of spurious error contained in a digital (or analog) signal that confounds the true (transmitted) signal. In analysis, the term is synonymous with common data problems such as missing values, out-of-range values, alphanumeric transpositions, as well as spurious data features that are sample specific and not representative of population parameters.

Output: The result of a single neuron's processing of an input vector. In trained feed-forward networks, if the single neuron is in the first (input) layer or any hidden layer, the output becomes the input of the next neuron. If the single neuron happens to be in the last (output) layer of the network, this value is the network estimate of the dependent variable.

Perceptron: An early theoretical model of the neuron developed by Rosenblatt (1958) that was the first to incorporate a learning rule. The term is also used as a generic label for all trained feed-forward networks, which is often referred to collectively as multilayer perceptron networks.

Self-Organizing Maps (SOMs): A type of unsupervised neural network used to group similar cases in a sample. SOMs are unsupervised (see supervised network) in that they do not require a known dependent variable. They are typically used for exploratory analysis and to reduce dimensionality as an aid to interpretation of complex data. SOMs are similar in purpose to *k*-means clustering and factor analysis.

Stochastic Approximation: Using a statistical model to fit the probability distribution of a dependent variable given a set of independent predictors (see *deterministic model*).

Supervised Network: A neural network developed to predict a dependent variable from a given set of independent variables by exposing the network to sample cases consisting of matched dependent and independent variables. Supervised network training requires data containing known, correct values of an output associated with specific input variables for each sample case.

Topological Map: A two-dimensional diagram showing the relative position of sample cases mapped from a higher dimensional space to reveal similarity, dissimilarity, density, and natural clusters in the data.

Training: The process used to configure an artificial neural network by repeatedly exposing it to sample data. In feed-forward networks, as each incoming vector or individual input is processed, the network produces an output for that case. With each pass of every case vector in a sample (see *epoch*), connection weights between neurons are modified. A typical training regime may require tens to thousands of complete epochs before the network converges (see *convergence*).

Transfer Function: See *activation function*.

Unsupervised Network: A type of neural network used for mapping relationships in sample data while reducing dimensionality for interpretive simplicity. SOMs are unsupervised (see *supervised network*) in that they do not require a known dependent variable. They are typically used for exploratory analysis and interpretation of complex data rather than forecasting, estimation, or classification.

Validity Coefficient: A statistical measure of association, usually the Pearson product–moment correlation coefficient, that summarizes the direction and magnitude of the relationship between predictor variables (e.g., preemployment questionnaire data) and criterion measures of job performance.

REFERENCES

Ackley, D., Hinton, G., & Sejnowski, T. (1985). A learning algorithm for Boltzmann machines. *Cognitive Science, 9*, 147–169.

Aggarwal, A., Travers, S., & Scott-Conner, C. (2000). Selection of surgical residents: A neural network approach. *Cybernetics and Systems: An International Journal, 31*, 417–430.

Allen, N., & Meyer, J. (1990). The measurement and antecedents of affective, continuance and normative commitment to the organization. *Journal of Occupational Psychology, 63*, 1–18.

Anderson, J., & Rosenfeld, E. (2000). *Talking nets: An oral history of neural networks.* Cambridge, MA: MIT Press.

Asin, R. (2000). Neural networks: A science in trouble. *ACM SIGKDD Newsletter, 1*, 33–38.

Austin, J., Scherbaum, C., & Mahlman, R. (2002). History of research methods in industrial and organizational psychology: Measurement, design, analysis. In S. Rogelberg (Ed.), *Handbook of research methods in industrial and organizational psychology* (pp. 3–33). Oxford, England: Blackwell.

Autor, D., & Scarborough, D. (2004). *Will job testing harm minority workers?* (Working Paper No. 10763). Cambridge, MA: National Bureau of Economic Research.

Axelrod, N. N. (1999). Embracing technology: The application of complexity theory to business. *Strategy and Leadership, 27*, 56–58.

Baatz, E. B. (1995). Making brain waves. *CIO Executive, 9*(7), 23–29.

Bailey, J. (1996). *After thought: The computer challenge to human intelligence.* New York: HarperCollins.

Bain, A. (1873). *Mind and body: Theories of their relation.* New York: Appleton.

Beaty, J., Fallon, J., & Shepherd, W. (2002, April). Proctored versus unproctored Web-based administration of a cognitive ability test. In F. L. Oswald & J. M. Stanton (Chairs), *Virtually hired? The implications of Web-based testing for personnel selection.* Symposium conducted at the annual meeting of the Society for Industrial and Organizational Psychology, Toronto, Ontario, Canada.

Becker, H. (1960). Notes on the concept of commitment. *American Journal of Sociology, 66*, 32–42.

Becker, T., & Billings, R. (1996). Profiles of commitment: An empirical test. *Journal of Organizational Behavior, 14*, 177–190.

Bettis, R. A., & Prahalad, C. K. (1995). The dominant logic: Retrospective and extension. *Strategic Management Journal, 16*, 5–14.

Bigby, D. (1992). *Tailored customer service selection systems for "a large service organization in the Southwest": Phase I. Sales agents technical report.* Dallas, TX: Bigby, Havis & Associates.

Bird, A., Gunz, H., & Arthur, M. B. (2002). Careers in a complex world: The search for new perspectives in the new science. *Management, 5,* 1–14.

Blalock, H. (1961). *Causal inferences in non-experimental research.* New York: Norton.

Bluedorn, A. (1982). The theories of turnover: Causes, effects and meaning. In S. Barcharach (Ed.), *Research in the sociology of organizations* (pp. 75–128). Greenwich, CT: JAI Press.

Buchanan, B. (1974). Building organizational commitment: The socialization of managers in work organizations. *Administrative Science Quarterly, 19,* 533–546.

Bunge, M. A (1967). *Scientific research: I. The search for system.* Berlin, Germany: Springer-Verlag.

Bylinsky, G. (1993, September 6). Computers that learn by doing. *Fortune, 128,* 96–102.

Caldwell, D., Chatman, J., & O'Reilly, C. (1990). Building organizational commitment: A multi-firm study. *Journal of Occupational Psychology, 63,* 245–261.

Carson, K. D., Carson, P. P., Roe, C. W., Birkenmeier, B. J., & Phillips, J. S. (1999). Four commitment profiles and their relationships to empowerment, service recovery and work attitudes. *Public Personnel Management, 28,* 1–11.

Caudill, M. (1990). *Naturally intelligent systems.* Cambridge, MA: MIT Press.

Caudill, M. (1991). Neural network training tips and techniques. *AI Expert, 6,* 56–61.

Caudill, M., & Butler, C. (1992). *Understanding neural networks: Computer explorations.* Cambridge, MA: MIT Press.

Chambless, B., & Scarborough, D. (2001). Information theoretic feature selection for neural network training. *Proceedings of the International Joint Conference on Neural Networks, 11,* 1443–1448.

Chryssolouris, G., Lee, M., & Ramsey, A. (1996). Confidence interval prediction for neural network models. *IEEE Transactions on Neural Networks, 7,* 229–232.

Cohen, J., & Cohen, P. (1983). *Applied multiple regression/correlation analysis for the behavioral sciences.* Hillsdale, NJ: Erlbaum.

Collins, B. (2000, December). *Driving out statistical results with neural nets.* Paper presented at the Visionary Marketing for the 21st Century Forum of the Australia New Zealand Management Association Conference, Sydney, Australia.

Collins, J. M., & Clark, M. R. (1993) An application of the theory of neural computation to the prediction of workplace behavior: An illustration and assessment of network analysis. *Personnel Psychology, 46,* 503–524.

Conover, W. (1980). *Practical nonparametric statistics* (2nd ed.). New York: Wiley.

Cox, E. (1995). *Fuzzy logic for business and industry.* Rockland, MA: Charles River Media.

Crevier, D. (1993). *AI: The tumultuous history of the search for artificial intelligence.* New York: HarperCollins.

Deboeck, G., & Kohonen, T. (1998). *Visual explorations in finance with self-organizing maps.* Berlin, Germany: Springer-Verlag.

Depsey, J., Folchi, J., & Sands, W. (1995). *Comparison of alternative types of prediction models for personnel attrition* (Human Resources Research Organization Tech. Rep. No. FR-PRD-95-05). San Diego, CA: Navy Personnel Research and Development Center.

Detienne, K., Detienne, D., & Joshie, S. (2003). Neural networks as statistical tools for business researchers. *Organizational Research Methods, 6,* 236–265.

Detienne, K., Lewis, L., & Detienne, D. (2003). Artificial neural networks for the management researcher: The state of the art. *The Forum: A Publication of the Research Methods Division of the Academy of Management, 8,* 1–18.

Dickieson, J., & Gollub, L. (1992). *Artificial neural networks and training.* Unpublished manuscript, Navy Personnel Research and Development Center, San Diego, CA.

Dickieson, J., & Wilkins, C. (1992). An exploratory examination of artificial neural networks as an alternative to linear regression. In *Independent research and exploratory development programs: FY91 annual report* (NPRDC No. 19-92-5, pp. 65–71). San Diego, CA: Navy Personnel Research and Development Center.

Dispenza, G., & Dasgupta, C. (1992, June). *Comparisons between neural network models and multivariate statistical techniques for marketing research analysis.* Paper presented at the Advanced Research Techniques Forum of the American Marketing Association, Lake Tahoe, NV.

Dunnette, M. (1963). A modified model for test validation and selection research. *Journal of Applied Psychology, 47,* 317–323.

Dutta, S., & Shekhar, S. (1988). Bond-rating: A non conservative application of neural networks. *Proceedings of the IEEE International Conference on Neural Networks, 2,* 443–450.

Edwards, J. E., & Parry, M. E. (1993). On the use of polynomial regression equations as an alternative to difference scores in organizational research. *Academy of Management Journal, 36,* 1577–1614.

Einstein, A. (1940). The fundaments of theoretical physics. In C. Seelig (Ed.), *Ideas and opinions by Albert Einstein* (pp. 223–335). New York: Wings Books.

Equal Employment Opportunity Commission, Civil Service Commission, Department of Labor, and Department of Justice. (1978). Uniform guidelines on employee selection procedures. *Federal Register, 43*(166), 38295–38309.

Eudaptics. (2001). *Viscovery SOMine Version 4.0: Users manual.* Vienna, Austria: Author.

Fahlman, S. (1988). *An empirical study of learning speed in backpropagation neural networks* (CMU Tech. Rep. No. 6 SMU-CS:82-162). Pittsburgh, PA: Carnegie Mellon University.

Fensterstock, A. (2001). Credit scoring: The application of neural networks to credit scoring. *Business Credit, 103,* 58–61.

Friedman, J. (1991). Multivariate adaptive regression splines. *Annals of Statistics, 19,* 1–141.

Fromkin, H. L., & Sherwood, J. J. (Eds.). (1974). *Integrating the organization: A social psychological analysis*. New York: Free Press.

Galvani, L. (1791). *De viribus electricitatis in motu musculari commentarius* [Commentary on the effect of electricity on muscular motion]. Retrieved January 18, 2006, from http://www.cis.unibo.it/cis13b/bsco3/intro_opera.asp?id_opera=23

Garavaglia, S. (1993). Interpreting neural network output: Informational signals. *PC Artificial Intelligence, 7,* 3.

Garson, D. G. (1991a). A comparison of neural network and expert systems algorithms with common multivariate procedures for analysis of social science data. *Social Science Computer Review, 9,* 399–434.

Garson, D. G. (1991b). Interpreting neural net connection weights. *AI Expert,* 6(4), 47–51.

Garson, D. G. (1998). *Neural networks: An introductory guide for social scientists.* London: Sage.

Glaser, B., & Strauss, A. L. (1967). *The discovery of grounded theory: Strategies for qualitative research.* Chicago: Aldine.

Glatzer, H. (1992, August 10). Neural networks take on real world problems. *ComputerWorld,* 21.

Gosling, S., Vazire, S., Srivastava, S., & John, O. (2004). Should we trust Web-based studies: A comparative analysis of six preconceptions about Internet questionnaires. *American Psychologist, 59,* 93–104.

Green, B. P., & Choi, J. H. (1997). Assessing the risk of management fraud through neural network technology. *Auditing, 16,* 4–29.

Guion, R. (1992a). Agenda for research and action. In P. Smith (Ed.), *Job satisfaction: How people feel about their jobs and how it affects their performance* (pp. 257–281). New York: Lexington Books.

Guion, R. (1992b). Personnel assessment, selection, and placement. In M. D. Dunnette & L. M. Hough (Eds.), *Handbook of industrial and organizational psychology* (2nd ed., Vol. 2, p. 367). Palo Alto, CA: Consulting Psychologists Press.

Guion, R. (1998). *Assessment, measurement, and prediction for personnel decisions.* Mahwah, NJ: Erlbaum.

Handler, C., & Hunt, S. (2003). *Rocket-Hire buyer's guide to online screening and staffing assessment systems.* Saint John, WA: PubSync.

Hanges, P. J., Lord, R. G., & Dickson, M. W. (2000). An information processing perspective on leadership and culture: A case for connectionist architecture. *Applied Psychology: An International Review, 49,* 133–161.

Hanges, P., Lord, R., Godfrey, E., & Raver, J. (2002). "Modeling nonlinear relationships: Neural networks and catastrophe analysis." In S. Rogelberg (Ed.), *Handbook of research methods in industrial and organizational psychology* (pp. 431–455). Malden, MA: Blackwell.

Hanisch, K. A., Hulin, C. L., & Seitz, S. T. (1996). Mathematical/computational modeling of organizational withdrawal processes: Benefits, methods, results. In

G. Ferris (Ed.), *Research in personnel and human resources management* (Vol. 14, pp. 91–142). Greenwich, CT: JAI Press.

Hastie, T., Tibshirani, R., & Friedman, J. (2001). *The elements of statistical learning: Data mining, inference and prediction.* New York: Springer-Verlag.

Haykin, S. (1994). *Neural networks: A comprehensive foundation.* New York: Macmillan.

Haykin, S. (1999). *Neural networks: A comprehensive foundation.* Upper Saddle River, NJ: Prentice Hall.

Hays, W. L. (1988). *Statistics* (4th ed.). New York: Holt, Rinehart & Winston.

Hebb, D. (1949). *The organization of behavior.* New York: Wiley.

Hopfield, J. (1982). Neural networks and physical systems with emergent collective computational abilities. *Proceedings of the National Academy of Sciences, 79,* 2554–2558.

Howell, W. (1991). Human factors in the workplace. In M. Dunnette, L. Hough, & H. Triandis (Eds.), *Handbook of industrial and organizational psychology* (2nd ed., pp. 209–269). Palo Alto, CA: Consulting Psychologists Press.

Hunt, E. (2002). *Thoughts on thought.* Mahwah, NJ: Erlbaum.

Hunt, J. G., & Ropo, A. U. (2003). Longitudinal organizational research and the third scientific discipline. *Group & Organization Management, 28,* 315–340.

Hunt, S., Gibby, R., Hemingway, M., Irwin, J., Scarborough, D., & Truxillo, D. (2004, April). *Internet pre-screening: Does it lead to better hiring decisions?* Paper presented at the annual meeting of the Society for Industrial and Organizational Psychology, Chicago, IL.

Iaffaldano, M., & Muchinsky, P. (1985). Job satisfaction and job performance: A meta-analysis. *Psychological Bulletin, 97,* 251–273.

Jacobs, R. (1988). Increased rates of convergence through learning rate adaptation. *Neural Networks, 1,* 295–307.

James, W. (1890). *The principles of psychology.* New York: Thoemmes Press.

Jick, T. D. (1979). Mixing qualitative and quantitative methods: Triangulation in action. *Administrative Science Quarterly, 24,* 602–634.

Kane, J., & Freeman, K. A. (1986). MBO and performance appraisal: A mixture that's not a solution, Part 1. *Personnel Journal, 63,* 26–36.

Kaplan, A. (1964). *The conduct of inquiry: Methodology for behavioral science.* San Francisco: Chandler.

Kaufman, S. A. (1993). *The origins of order: Self-organization and sections in evolution.* New York: Oxford University Press.

Kaufman, S. A. (1995). *At home in the universe: The search for laws of self-organization and complexity.* New York: Oxford University Press.

Kelman, H. (1958). Compliance, identification and internalization: Three processes of attitude change. *Journal of Conflict Resolution, 2,* 51–60.

Kiang, M. Y., & Kumar, A. (2001). An evaluation of self-organizing map networks as a robust alternative to factor analysis in data mining applications. *Information Systems Research, 9,* 177–184.

Kierkegaard, S. (1992). *Concluding unscientific postscript.* Princeton, NJ: Princeton University Press.

Kim, J. O. (1978). *Factor analysis: Statistical methods and practical issues.* Newbury Park, CA: Sage.

Klimasauskas, C. C. (1991). *Applications in neural computing.* Pittsburgh, PA: NeuralWare, Inc.

Kohonen, T. (1982). Self-organized formation of topologically correct feature maps. *Biological Cybernetics, 43,* 59–69.

Kohonen, T. (1995). *Self-organizing maps.* Berlin, Germany: Springer-Verlag.

Kollicker, A. K. (1853). *Manual of human histology* (G. Busk & T. Huxley, Trans.). London: Sydenham Society.

Kopelman, R., Rovenpor, J., & Millsap, R. (1992). Rationale and construct validity evidence for the Job Search Behavior Index: Because intentions (and New Year's resolutions) often come to naught. *Journal of Vocational Behavior, 40,* 269–287.

Kosko, B. (1992). *Neural networks and fuzzy systems: A dynamical systems approach to machine intelligence.* Englewood Cliffs, NJ: Prentice Hall.

Kosko, B. (1993). *Fuzzy thinking: The new science of fuzzy logic.* New York: Hyperion Books.

Kraut, R., Olson, J., Banaji, M., Bruckman, A., Cohen, J., & Couper, M. (2004). Psychological research on-line: Report of Board of Scientific Affairs' Advisory Group on the conduct of research on the Internet. *American Psychologist, 59,* 105–117.

Lapedes, A., & Farber, R. (1987). *Nonlinear signal processing using neural networks: Prediction and systems modeling* (Los Alamos National Laboratory Tech. Rep. No. LA-UR-87-2662). Los Alamos, NM: Los Alamos National Laboratory.

Lawler, E. E. (1967). The multitrait–multimethod approach to measuring job performance. *Journal of Applied Psychology, 51,* 369–381.

Lawrence, J. (1993). *Introduction to neural networks: Design, theory, and applications* (5th ed.). Nevada City, CA: California Scientific Software Press.

Le Cun, Y. (1985). Une procedure d'apprentissage pour reseau a seuil assymetrique [A learning procedure for asymmetric threshold networks]. *Proceedings Cognitiva, 85,* 599–604.

Lee, C., & Marshall, R. (1998). Measuring influence in the family decision making process using an observational method. *Qualitative Market Research: An International Journal, 1,* 88–98.

Lee, C., Rey, T., Mentele, J., & Garver, M. (2005, April). *Structured neural network techniques for modeling loyalty and profitability.* Paper presented at the Data Mining and Predictive Modeling Forum of SUGI (SAS Users Group International), Philadelphia, PA.

Lee, T. W., & Mitchell, T. R. (1994). An alternative approach: The unfolding model of voluntary employee turnover. *Academy of Management Review, 19,* 51–90.

Lee, T. W., & Mowday, R. T. (1987). Voluntarily leaving an organization: An empirical investigation of Steers and Mowday's model of turnover. *Academy of Management Journal, 30,* 721–744.

Lefkowitz, J., Somers, M., & Weinberg, K. (1984). The role of need salience and/ or need level as moderators of the relationship between need satisfaction and work alienation–involvement. *Journal of Vocational Behavior, 24,* 142–158.

Leslie, L. M., & Hanges, P. (2005, April). *Factors affecting the utility of artificial neural networks.* Poster presented at the annual meeting of the Society for Industrial and Organizational Psychology, Los Angeles, CA.

Lykins, S., & Chance, D. (1992, March). Comparing artificial neural networks and multiple regression for predictive application. *Proceedings of the Eighth Annual Conference on Applied Mathematics* (pp. 155–169). Edmond: University of Central Oklahoma.

Marshall, D., & English, D. (2000). Neural network modeling of risk assessment in child protective services. *Psychological Methods, 5,* 102–124.

Mathews, M., White, M. C., & Long, R. G. (1999). Why study the complexity sciences in the social sciences. *Human Relations, 52,* 439–462.

McCulloch, W., & Pitts, W. (1943). A logical calculus of the ideas immanent in nervous activity. *Bulletin of Mathematical Biophysics, 5,* 115–133.

McElroy, M. W. (2000). Integrating complexity theory, knowledge management, and organizational learning. *Journal of Knowledge Management, 4,* 195–203.

Medsker, L., & Liebowitz, J. (1994). *Design and development of expert systems and neural networks.* New York: Macmillan.

Meissner, G., & Kawano, N. (2001). Capturing the volatility smile of options on high-tech stocks: A combined GARCH–neural network approach. *Journal of Economics and Finance, 25,* 276–293.

Meyer, J., & Allen, N. (1984). Testing the "side-bet" theory of organizational commitment: Some methodological concerns. *Journal of Applied Psychology, 69,* 372–378.

Minsky, M., & Papert, S. (1969). *Perceptrons.* Cambridge, MA: MIT Press.

Mowday, R., Steers, R., & Porter, L. (1982). *Employee–organization linkages: The psychology of commitment, absenteeism and turnover.* New York: Academic Press.

Mumford, M., Snell, A., & Reiter-Palmon, R. (1994). Personality and background data: Life history and self-concepts in an ecological system. In G. S. Stokes, M. D. Mumford, & W. A. Owens (Eds.), *Biodata handbook: Theory, research, and use of biographical information in selection and performance prediction* (pp. 583–616). Palo Alto, CA: Consulting Psychologists Press.

Munsterberg, H. (1913). *Psychology and industrial efficiency.* Boston: Houghton Mifflin.

Nam, K. D., & Prybutok, V. R. (1992). A comparison of a neural network approach to linear and quadratic discriminant analysis in the two group problem. *Proceedings of the Decision Sciences Institute, 2*, 1033–1035.

NeuralWare, Inc. (1994). *NeuralWorks Professional II Plus.* Pittsburgh, PA: Author.

NeuralWare, Inc. (2004). *NeuralWorks Predict Version 5.1.* Pittsburgh, PA: Author.

Nickels, B. (1994). The nature of biodata. In G. S. Stokes, M. D. Mumford, & W. A. Owens (Eds.), *Biodata handbook: Theory, research, and use of biographical information in selection and performance prediction* (pp. 1–14). Palo Alto, CA: Consulting Psychologists Press.

Olcay, B. (1999). Extracting decision trees from trained neural networks. *Proceedings of the ACM SIGKDD International Conference on Knowledge Discovery and Data Mining,* 456–461.

O'Reilly, C. A (1991). Organizational behavior: Where we've been, where we're going. *Annual Review of Psychology, 42*, 427–458.

Ostberg, D. (2005). *A comparative analysis of artificial neural networks, classification trees and multivariate linear regression for predicting retail employee tenure and turnover.* Unpublished doctoral dissertation, University of Portland.

Palocsay, S., & White, M. (2004). Network modeling in cross-cultural research: A comparison with multiple regression. *Organizational Research Methods, 7*, 389–399.

Parker, D. (1985). *Learning logic* (Tech. Rep. No. 47). Cambridge, MA: MIT Center for Computational Research in Economics and Management Science.

Ployhart, R., Weekley, J., Holtz, B., & Kemp, C. (2002, April). Web-based versus paper-and-pencil testing: A comparison of factor structures across applicants and incumbents. In F. Oswald & J. Stanton (Chairs), *Virtually hired? The implications of Web-based testing for personnel selection.* Symposium conducted at the annual meeting of the Society for Industrial and Organizational Psychology, Toronto, Ontario, Canada.

Porter, L., Steers, R., Mowday, R., & Boulian, P. (1974). Organizational commitment, job satisfaction and turnover among psychiatric technicians. *Journal of Applied Psychology, 59*, 603–609.

Quinn, R., & Staines, G. (1979). *The 1977 Quality of Employment Survey.* Ann Arbor: University of Michigan, Institute for Social Research.

Rakes, T. R., Kohers, G., Slade, M. B., & Rees, L. P. (1990). An artificial intelligence approach to the two-group discriminant analysis problem. *Proceedings of the Southeast Decision Sciences Institute,* 119–121.

Randall, D. (1987). Commitment and the organization: The organization man revisited. *Academy of Management Review, 12*, 460–471.

Rappa, M., & Debackere, K. (1992). Technological communities and the diffusion of knowledge. *R & D Management, 22*, 209–220.

Rashevesky, N. (1935). Outline of a physico–mathematical theory of the brain. *General Psychology, 13*, 82–112.

Reed, R., & Marks, R. (1999). *Neural smithing: Supervised learning in feedforward artificial neural networks.* Cambridge, MA: MIT Press.

Reichers, A. (1986). Conflict and organizational commitments. *Journal of Applied Psychology, 71,* 508–514.

Ripley, B. (1996). *Pattern recognition and neural networks.* Cambridge, England: Cambridge University Press.

Rizzo, J., House, R., & Lirtzman, S. (1970). Role conflict and ambiguity in complex organizations. *Administrative Science Quarterly, 15,* 150–163.

Rosenblatt, F. (1958). The perceptron: A probabilistic model for information storage and organization in the brain. *Psychological Review, 65,* 386–408.

Rucci, A., & Tweney, R. (1980). Analysis of variance and the "second discipline" of scientific psychology: A historical account. *Psychological Bulletin, 87,* 166–184.

Rumelhart, D., Hinton, G., & Williams, R. (1986). *Parallel distributed processing: Vol. 1. Explorations in the microstructure of cognition.* Cambridge, MA: MIT Press.

Sands, W. A. (1992). Artificial neural networks: A tool for psychologists. *Proceedings of the 33rd Annual Conference of the Military Testing Association, 33,* 284–388.

Sands, W. A., & Wilkins, C. (1991). Artificial neural networks for personnel selection. *Proceedings of the 33rd Annual Conference of the Military Testing Association, 33,* 389–392.

Sands, W. A., & Wilkins, C. A. (1992). A comparison of artificial neural networks and linear regression for dichotomous criterion prediction. *Independent research and independent exploratory development: FY91 Annual Report* (Admin. Pub. No. 92-5, pp. 73–78). San Diego, CA: Navy Personnel Research and Development Center.

Scarborough, D. (1995). *An evaluation of backpropagation neural network modeling as an alternative methodology for criterion validation of employee selection testing.* Unpublished doctoral dissertation, University of North Texas.

Scarborough, D. (2002). *Paper vs. electronic hiring procedures: A cross-company comparison on three metrics of workforce quality* (Tech. Rep.). Beaverton, OR: Unicru, Inc.

Scarborough, D. (2004). *Conversation with the former vice president of loss prevention for a national retailer* (Forum: Think Tank 2.1). Tampa, FL: King Rogers International Inc.

Scarborough, D., & Somers, M. (2002, April). Dust bowl empiricism on steroids: A data mining approach to employee selection. In N. Dyer & P. Hanges (Chairs), *The real AI: Artificial neural networks, statistics, and psychological theory.* Symposium conducted at the annual meeting of the Society for Industrial and Organizational Psychology, Toronto, Ontario, Canada.

Schmidt, F., & Hunter, H. (1998). The validity and utility of selection methods in personnel psychology: Practical and theoretical implications of 85 years of research findings. *Psychological Bulletin, 124,* 262–274.

Schrodt, P. (1991). Prediction of interstate conflict outcomes using a neural network. *Social Science Computer Review, 9,* 359–380.

Schwartz, E. I. (1992, November 2). Where neural networks are already at work. *Business Week*, 136–137.

Scott, W. (1969). *Human efficiency in business: A contribution to the psychology of business.* Bristol, England: Thoemmes Press. (Original work published 1911)

Sharda, R., & Patil, R. B. (1992). Connectionist approach to time-series prediction: An empirical test. *Journal of Intelligent Manufacturing, 3,* 317–323.

Short, D., & Yerex, R. (2002). *Longitudinal analysis of tenure predictor effects on average length of service* (Tech. Rep.). Beaverton, OR: Unicru, Inc.

Sinar, E., Paquet, S., & Scott, D. (2002, April). *Internet versus paper selection tests: Exploring comparability issues.* Poster presented at the annual meeting of the Society for Industrial and Organizational Psychology, Toronto, Ontario, Canada.

Smith, P. (1976). Behaviors, results, and organizational effectiveness: The problem of criteria. In M. D. Dunnette (Ed.), *Handbook of industrial and organizational psychology* (pp. 745–775). Chicago: Rand-McNally.

Somers, M. J. (1999) Application of two neural network paradigms to the study of voluntary employee turnover. *Journal of Applied Psychology, 84,* 177–185.

Somers, M. J. (2000, April). *Self-organizing maps and commitment profiles.* Poster presented at the annual meeting of the Society for Industrial and Organizational Psychology, New Orleans, LA.

Somers, M. J. (2001). Thinking differently: Assessing nonlinearities in the relationship between work attitudes and job performance using a Bayesian neural network. *Journal of Occupational and Organizational Psychology, 74,* 47–62.

Stanton, J., Sederburg, M., & Smith, P. (2000, April). *Applying neural networking techniques to prediction problems in I-O psychology.* Poster presented at the annual meeting of the Society for Industrial and Organizational Psychology, New Orleans, LA.

Starbuck, W. H., & Mezias, J. M. (1996). Opening Pandora's box: Studying the accuracy of managers' perceptions. *Journal of Organizational Behavior, 17,* 99–117.

StatSoft, Inc. (2002). *Neural networks in STATISTICA 6.0.* Tulsa, OK: Author.

StatSoft, Inc. (2003a). *Neural networks in STATISTICA 7.0.* Tulsa, OK: Author.

StatSoft, Inc. (2003b). *STATISTICA Version 6.1.* Tulsa, OK: Author.

Stigler, S. (1999). *Statistics on the table: The history of statistical concepts and methods.* Cambridge, MA: Harvard University Press.

Sturt, G. (1923). *The wheelwright's shop.* Cambridge, England: Cambridge University Press.

Surkan, A. J., & Singleton, J. C. (1990). Neural networks for bond rating improved by multiple hidden layers. *International Joint Conference on Neural Networks,* 157–162.

Swingler, K. (1996). *Applying neural networks: A practical guide.* New York: Academic Press.

Tang, Z., Almeida, C., & Fishwick, P. (1990). Time series forecasting using neural networks vs. Box–Jenkins methodology. *Proceedings of the First Workshop on Neural Networks: Academic/Industrial/NASA/Defense, 1,* 95–100.

Thissen-Roe, A. (2005). *Adaptive selection of personality items to inform a neural network predicting job performance.* Unpublished doctoral dissertation, University of Washington.

von Altrock, C. (1996). *Fuzzy logic and neurofuzzy applications in business and finance.* Upper Saddle River, NJ: Prentice Hall.

Walker, I., & Milne, S. (2005). Exploring function estimators as an alternative to regression in psychology. *Behavior Research Methods, 37,* 23–36.

Wang, P. (2001). *Computing with words.* New York: Wiley.

Ward Systems Group, Inc. (1993). *Neural network demonstrations.* (Available from Ward Systems Group, Inc., Executive Park West, Hillcrest Drive, Frederick, MD 21702)

Wasserman, P. D. (1989). *Neural computing: Theory and practice.* New York: Van Nostrand Reinhold.

Werbos, P. (1974). *Beyond regression: New tools for prediction and analysis in the behavioral sciences.* Unpublished doctoral dissertation, Harvard University.

West, B. J. (1980). *Lecture notes in biomathematics: An essay on the importance of being nonlinear.* Berlin, Germany: Springer-Verlag.

Westbury, C., Buchanan, L., Sanderson, M., Rhemtulla, M., & Phillips, L. (2003). Using genetic programming to discover nonlinear variable interactions. *Behavior Research Methods, Instruments, and Computers, 35,* 202–216.

White, H. (1989a). Learning in artificial neural networks: A statistical perspective. *Neural Computation, 1,* 425–464.

White, H. (1989b). Neural network learning and statistics. *AI Expert, 4,* 48–52.

White, M., Marin, D., Brazeal, D. V., & Friedman, W. H. (1997). The evolution of organizations: Suggestions from complexity theory about the interplay between natural selection and adaptation. *Human Relations, 50,* 1383–1401.

Widrow, B., & Hoff, M. E. (1960). Adaptive switching circuits. *WES-CON Convention Record, 4,* 96.

Wiener, Y. (1982). Commitment in organizations: A normative view. *Academy of Management Review, 7,* 418–428.

Williams, R., & Herrup, K. (1988). The control of neuron number. *Annual Review of Neuroscience, 11,* 423–453.

Willshaw, D., & von der Malsburg, C. (1973). How patterned neural connections can be set up by self-organization. *Proceedings of the Royal Society of London Series B, 194,* 431–435.

Ye, N. (Ed.). (2003). *The handbook of data mining.* Mahwah, NJ: Erlbaum.

Yerex, R. (2005). *The incremental employee contribution model* (Tech. Rep.). Beaverton, OR: Unicru, Inc.

Yerkes, R. R. (1921). *Memoirs of the National Academy of Sciences: Vol. XV. Psychological examining in the United States Army.* Washington, DC: U.S. Government Printing Office.

Yoon, Y., Swales, G., & Margavio, T. M. (1993). A comparison of discriminant analysis versus artificial neural networks. *Journal of the Operational Research Society, 44,* 51–60.

Zadeh, L. (1965). Fuzzy sets. *Information and Control, 8,* 338–353.

INDEX

Ackley, D., 38
Activation thresholds, 141
Adams, John Couch, 26
Adaptive gradient, 77
ADELINE (adaptive linear element),
    33–36
Algorithms
    pattern recognition, 52, 61, 142–143
    self-modifying, 28
Allen, N., 125, 128
Alternative models, evaluating, 14–15,
    109–110
Ambiguity, of theoretical basis, 106
Anderson, J., 40
ANNs. See Artificial neural networks
    (ANNs)
Applied research, ANNs and, 3–4, 17,
    43, 58–59
Architecture, network. See Network
    architecture
Artificial intelligence, 28
Artificial neural network, use of term, 12,
    61
Artificial neural networks (ANNs). See
    also Employee selection research;
    Neural network paradigms;
    Neural networks, types of; Neural
    network software; Nonlinearity;
    Organizational research
    applications, 3–4, 17, 43, 58–59
    as black boxes, 138, 140
    and complexity theory, 56–57
    considerations for use, 14–17,
        127–128
    and conventional statistical
        methods, 45, 49, 58, 61, 81–82,
        90–94, 121–122, 141–143, 154
    exploratory use, 51–56, 148–150
    limitations, 137–140
    in organizational research, 45–46,
        155–157
    as pattern recognition algorithms,
        52, 61, 142–143

and statistics, 90–94
    as theory development tool, 48–52
Associative memories, 28
Astronomy, 21, 23
Austin, J., 26

Babbage, Charles, 26
Backpropagation, 14n, 37–40, 42, 71–73.
    See also Neural networks, types of
Backpropagation training algorithms
    (generalized delta rule), 38–39
Bailey, J., 40
Bain, Alexander, 29–30
Bases of commitment, 124
Basins of attraction, 38
Batch processing, 114
Becker, H., 124
Becker, T., 125–126
Behavior
    causes not directly observable, 22
    measurement of, 22–24
    observation of, 22–23
Behavioral research in organizations. See
    Organizational research
Behavioral science
    development of, 21–24
    use of term, 24–25
Bettis, R. A., 47–48
Bias
    in criterion measures, 109
    and data mining, 108–109
    illegal, 121
    perceptual, 23
Bidirectional associative memory
    network, 40
Billings, R., 125–126
Biodata, 16, 106–107
Biology, and neural network theory,
    30–33
Biology metaphor, used for ANNs,
    12–12n
Black boxes, ANNs as, 138, 140
Bluedorn, A., 128

Bond rating prediction, 91
Boundary conditions, 55
Box–Jenkins methodology, 92
Brain, human, 22
Brain activity, measurement of, 22
Brain imaging technology, 22
Brittleness, 17n, 107n
Business administration, and neural
    networks, 90–91

Call center employees, 111–117
Carson, K. D., 126
Cascade-correlation paradigm, 72
Cascade optimization, 43
Caudill, M., 73
Causal inferences, assigning, 116–117
Chambless, B., 154
Chance, D., 94–95
Channeled relationships, 54, 150
Clark, M. R., 16, 95, 97, 107
Classification, 61, 67, 71–81, 91, 94–96
Classification tree, 92, 96
Clinical psychology, and neural networks,
    94–95
Closed-loop employee records, 102,
    118–119
Cluster analysis, 125
    SOMs and, 68–71
Clustering, 25, 61, 64, 67, 70, 123,
    126–127
Collins, B., 154
Collins, J. M., 16, 95, 97, 107
Commitment. See also Organizational
    commitment
    affective, 124
    continuance, 124
    foci and bases of, 124
    normative, 124
Commitment profiles, 125–126, 130–134
    study methodology, 128–129
    study rationale, 127–128
    use of clustering techniques,
        126–127
Competitive learning, in neural network
    theory, 37
Complexity, of data, 106–107
Complexity theory, 56–57
Compliance, as basis of commitment,
    124–125
Comprehensive models, 46, 51

Computational techniques, "brute force,"
    12
Computer, use of term, 26
Computer memory, active, 6–7
Computer modem technology, 34
Computer science, 28
Computer software, for neural networks,
    42, 76, 89, 141. See also Com-
        puter software programs; Internet
    demonstration versions, 63, 66
    documentation, 66
    graphical capabilities, 63
    integrated with statistical software,
        65–66
    platforms, 66–67
    price, 65
    selecting, 62–67
    stand-alone, 65–66
    tutorials, 146
    utilities, 109
Computer software engineering, 27
Computer software programs, 4, 43
    Eudaptics SOMine, 70
    Excel, 63
    LISREL, 57
    MATLAB, 64–65
    NeuralWare Predict, 42
    SAS, 65
    SPSS, 65, 129
    STATISTICA Neural Networks, 42,
        64–65, 129
Computing, history of, 26–28
Computing platforms, 66–67
    Linux, 66
    Macintosh, 66–67, 129
    UNIX, 66
    Windows, 66, 129
Configural scoring models, 112–113
Confirmatory factor analysis, 123
Confirmatory technique, ANNs as, 48–50
Conjugate gradient descent, 77, 112
Connectionist models, 28
Connection weight matrix, 107n, 112
    under delta rule, 35–36
    "jogging," 78
    and momentum, 77–78
Connection weights, 31–32
Consistency, assumption of, 47–48
Constructive approach, to network
    architecture, 71–72
Construct validity, 25

Consumer online behavior, 156
Continuous sigmoidal activation
    functions, 38
Conventional statistical methods, and
    ANNs, 45, 49, 58, 61, 81–82,
    90–94, 121–122, 141–143,
    154
Convergence, 38–39, 82, 112
Cornell University, 32
Cox, E., 155
Cred card activity monitoring, 156
Credit scoring models, 58, 62–63
Crevier, D., 40
Crew selection, naval, 97–100
Criteria, 103, 103n
Criterion fidelity, 105
Criterion validation, 97, 97n, 103–105
Cumulative delta rule, 76
Curve fitting, 51, 149
Customer loyalty, 154
Customer service representatives,
    119–120

Dasgupta, C., 92
Data, missing/noisy, 95, 107–108, 107n
Data collection, 11, 16. *See also* Data
    mining
Data mining, 15–16, 108–109, 119
Data processing, and information
    technology, 11–12
Data reduction, 67
    SOMs and, 68
Data sources, online, 11
Deboeck, G., 127
Delta rule, 34–36, 76
    cumulative, 76
    generalized, 38–39
    normalized cumulative, 76–77
Descartes, René, 20
Destructive approach, to network
    architecture, 71–72
Differential Factors Opinion
    Questionnaire, 96
Dimensionality. *See also* Surface response
    graphs
    in neural network theory, 35–38
    of SOMs, 68
Discriminant analysis, 67, 107n
Dispenza, G., 92
Dunnette, M., 104

Dutta, S., 90–91
Dynamic feedback, 38

Early adopters, 120–121
Echo cancellation, in long-distance tele-
    phone systems, 34
Edgeworth, Francis, 21, 23
Effects analysis, 92
Einstein, Albert, 20
Electrical engineering, and neural net-
    work theory, 33–36
Electronic survey data collection, 16
Empirical findings, and theoretical
    models, 48–52
Empiricism, 20–21, 28, 147, 149
Employee absenteeism, 128–129
Employee online behavior, 156. *See also*
    Internet
Employee records, closed-loop, 102,
    118–119
Employee selection networks (ESNs),
    110–122
    and equal employment opportunity,
    121–122
    trained to estimate length of service,
    117–121
    trained to estimate normalized sales
    revenue, 111–117
Employee selection research, 15–17, 43,
    96–100, 102–103, 105–122,
    155
Employee turnover, 117, 128, 148, 151.
    See also Organizational
    commitment
Employment discrimination, 121–122
Energy surfaces, 37–38, 82–85. *See also*
    Surface response graphs
English, D., 95
ENIAC (Electronic Numerical Integrator
    and Calculator), 26–27
Ensembles, of neural networks, 14,
    109–110
Equal employment opportunity, 121–122
Equilibrium, 82
Error term, 38–39. *See also* RMSE
    (root mean square error)
Error tolerance, 78
Eutrophication metaphor, in I/O
    psychology, 26
Experimental design, 23

Experimentation, to refine network
   architecture, 74
Expert systems, 92
Exploratory factor analysis, 26, 51, 70,
   123, 139
Exploratory studies, trend toward, 148–
   150, 155–156
Exploratory technique, ANNs as, 51–56

Fahlman, S., 72
Fairness, in employee selection, 121–122
Families, of neural networks, 109–110
Family decision-making processes, 154
Feature selection, 108, 154
Feedback loops, 40
Financial fraud detection, 58
Financial market behavior, 58
Fishing expedition, 51, 142
Flops (floating point operations per
   second), 27
Foci of commitment, 124
Formalization, 20
Fringe clusters, 70
Fringe factors, 70
Fuzzy set, use of term, 154
Fuzzy set theory, 154–155

Galileo, 20
Galton, Francis, 21
Galvani, Luigi, 29
Garson, D. G., 16, 89, 107, 116
Garver, M., 154
Gauss, Carl Friedrich, 23
Generalizability, 26, 106
Generalization, 73, 111, 138–139
Generalized delta rule, 38–39
General linear model, 25
Global minima, 38, 82
Graceful degradation, 100, 107n, 108
Gradient descent, 35–38, 76
Graphical analysis, 38
Graphical analysis, and data interpreta-
   tion, 82–85. See also Surface re-
   sponse graphs; Wire frame graphs
Group behavior, measurement of, 23
GUI (graphic user interface), 27
Guilford–Zimmerman Temperament
   Survey, 96
Guion, R., 48, 51, 53, 104, 149–150

Hanisch, K. A., 48
Hebb, Donald, 32
Hebb's law, 32
Heisenberg's uncertainty principle, 23
Heuristics, for neural network
   development, 43
Hidden clusters, 123
Hidden layers, 42–43, 71–72, 91, 139
Hidden units, 71–72, 91
Hierarchical cluster analysis, 67, 123
High fault tolerance, 107–108
Hinton, G., 37–38
History of science and technology, 19–21
Hoff, Ted, 33–36
Hopfield, John, 37
Hopfield network, 40
Hot spots, 140
House, R., 128
Hulin, C. L., 48
Human resource planning, 156
Hyperbolic tangent transfer function, 80

Identification, as basis of commitment,
   124–125
IEEE (Institute of Electrical and
   Electronics Engineers), 40
Independent holdout data, 111
Indeterminacy
   in conventional statistical analyses,
      139
   in neural computing paradigm,
      138–139
Industrial/organizational (I/O) psychol-
   ogy, development of, 25–26
Information technology (IT)
   and data processing, 11–12
   and employee selection, 101–102
   in social science, 26–28
Input layer, 42–43
Input vector, 37
Integration, of quantitative and qualita-
   tive research methodologies,
   146–148
Interactions, detecting and modeling,
   114–115
Interdisciplinary awareness, importance
   of, 24
Internalization, as basis of commitment,
   124–125
International Neural Network Society, 40

Internet, 27, 102, 107–108, 117–118, 156. *See also* Employee selection research
Internet applicant populations, 16, 107
Interpretation, of neural network behavior, 82–85, 140, 147–148, 152–153. *See also* Employee selection research
Item response theory, 25–26, 154

James, William, 30
Job analysis, 105
Job Descriptive Index, 97
job–person characteristics matrix, 104–105
job satisfaction–job performance relationship, 51, 149–150 modeling, 52–56
Journal of Applied Psychology, 25
Jury selection, 157

Kalman filter, 77
Kant, Immanuel, 20
Kaplan, A., 20
Kelman, H., 124
Kepler, Johannes, 20
Kierkegaard, S., 142
Klimasauskas, C. C., 72–73
k-means cluster analysis, 67, 96, 123 and SOMs, 129–133
Kohonen, Teuvo, 37, 68, 127
Kohonen networks, 41–42, 68, 96
Kolliker, Alexander, 29
Kosko, B., 20, 80, 155

Learn count, 77
Learning, in neural networks, 32, 63–64, 68, 141
Learning logic, 38
Learning rate, 77
Learning rule, 32, 78, 112
Le Cun, Y., 38
Lee, C., 154
Lee, T. W., 148, 151
Lefkowitz, J., 128
Legendre, Adrien, 26
Length of service, predicting, 109
Levenberg–Marquardt, 77

Limitations of ANNs, 137–140
interpretation, 140
network architectures, 139
preprocessing and outliers, 139–140
training, 138–139
Linear discriminant analysis, 91–92, 96
Linearity, 46–50, 78. *See also* Nonlinearity
Linear methods, and nonlinearity, 48
Linear regression, 92–93
Linear thresholding, 78
Lirtzman, S., 128
LMS (least mean square), 34–36. *See also* Delta rule
Local minima, 38
Logical positivism, 20–21
Logistic regression, 67, 90, 92, 95–96
Lovelace, Ada, 26
Lykins, S., 94–95

Machine intelligence, 28
MADELINE (multiple adaptive linear elements), 33–34
Management research, complexity theory in, 56
Mapping, 62–63, 84. *See also* Graphical analysis
Marketing, and ANNs, 92
Marks, R., 40
Marshall, D., 95
Mathematical models, and scientific method, 21
Mathematics
and history of science and technology, 20–21
and neural network theory, 38–40
McCulloch, Warren, 30–33
McCulloch–Pitts neuron, 30–32
McNemar test, 98, 100, 111
Measurement, 22–24, 57, 122, 143, 151
Measurement error, theory of, 23
Medicine, and neural network theory, 29–30
Memorization, 74, 110. *See also* Overtraining
Mentele, J., 154
Meta-analysis, 49, 53
Method-centrism, 3n
Meyer, J., 125, 128
Mezias, J. M., 47–48

Microprocesses, 150–152
Milne, S., 92–93
Minsky, Marvin, 36, 38
Mitchell, T. R., 148
MIT (Massachusetts Institute of
Technology), 36
MLPs (multilayer perceptrons), 71, 92–
93, 95–96
Model comparison studies, 93
Models
explanatory, 21
predictive, 21, 42
Moderated regression, 67
Momentum, 77–78
Mowday, R. T., 151
Multidimensional scaling, 25, 67–68
Multinomial logit model, 92
Multiple regression, 90–92, 96–97, 104,
107n, 151
Multivariate statistical methods, and
ANNs, 45, 49, 58, 61, 81–82,
90–94, 141–143, 154
Munsterberg, Hugo, 25
Myths concerning ANNs, 141–144

Nam, K. D., 91
Naval Personnel Research and Develop-
ment Center, San Diego, 97–
100
Nervous systems, mammalian, 22
Network architecture, 42–43, 91, 98,
129, 139
defining, 72–74
Networked computing, 27
Neural activation model, 30–32
Neural biology, 22
Neural computing paradigms, 66–67, 71
Neural modeling, 12–13
Neural network paradigms
included with software, 64
research testing, 153–154
selecting, 76–78
Neural networks. See Artificial neural
networks (ANNs)
Neural Networks, 40
Neural networks, types of, 40–42,
153–154
backpropagation, 38–40, 64, 80, 90–
92, 99, 112, 119
Bayesian, 54, 150

for employee selection, 110–122
feed-forward, 40, 42–43, 71–81,
155–156
functional link, 99–100
learning vector quantization, 71,
95–96
MLPs, 71
multiple-layer, 40
radial basis function, 42, 71
single-layer, 36, 40
supervised, 36, 40, 67, 71–81
unsupervised, 40–41, 67–71
Neural network software, 76, 89, 141. See
also Computer software programs
demonstration versions, 63, 66
documentation, 66
graphical capabilities, 63
integrated with statistical software,
65–66
platforms, 66–67
price, 65
selecting, 62–67
stand-alone, 65–66
tutorials, 146
utilities, 109
Neural network theory, 29
Neural validation modeling, 105–110
NeuralWare, Inc., 42
Neurons, self-organizing, 37
Nonlinear dependencies, SOMs and,
132–133
Nonlinear dynamics, in complexity
theory, 56
Nonlinearity, 47–53, 58, 78, 81, 104,
126–127, 134, 143, 146–150,
152
in job satisfaction–job performance
relationship, 52–56
Nonlinear regression, 90–93, 96. See also
Conventional statistical methods,
and ANNs
Normalized cumulative delta rule, 76–77
Nuclear energy production, 108

Observation, of behavior, 22–23
OLS (ordinary least squares) regression,
54, 67, 96, 98, 100, 140
Operating systems, 66–67
Operations research, and ANNs, 92
Opinion data, 109

Organization, use of term, 25
Organizational commitment, 124–134
Organizational psychology, 25, 95
Organizational research, 4–5, 24–26,
94–100
behavioral predictions, 94–100
and complexity theory, 56–57
linearity in, 46–47
and neural networks, 57–58, 64, 89–
90, 146–157
and predictive accuracy, 45–46
SOMs in, 123–124
Organizational research, applied, 58–59
Organizations, behavioral research in,
24–26
Ostberg, D., 96
Outliers, 74, 139–140
Output layer, 42–43
Overtraining, 52, 69–70, 76, 81, 110,
138–139, 142

Papert, Seymour, 36, 38
Parallel processing, 27
Parker, D., 38
Parsimony, principle of, 151
Path analysis, 92
Pattern recognition algorithms, ANNs as,
52, 61, 142–143
Patterns of organizational commitment,
124–126
Pearson, Karl, 21, 23
Pearson product–moment correlation
coefficient, 103
Perceptron convergence theorem,
Rosenblatt's, 33
Perceptron learning theorem,
Rosenblatt's, 32
Perceptrons, 32–33, 36, 78
multilayer (MLPs), 71, 92–93,
95–96
Perceptron training algorithm,
Rosenblatt's, 32–34
Personal computers (PCs), 27. *See also*
Computer software, for neural
networks; Internet
Personnel Psychology, 95
Phrenology, 30
Physical sciences, and neural networks,
30, 89
Pitts, Walter, 30–33

Placement, 156
Political science, and ANNs, 92
Power analysis, 25
Prahalad, C. K., 47–48
Prediction, 61, 67, 71–81, 91, 96–100
Predictive accuracy, 45–46
loss in, 80–81
Predictor–criterion fidelity, 106
Predictors, 102, 102n
Preprocessing of data, 65, 69, 78,
139–140
Process control, real-time, 34
Programming languages, 27. *See also*
Computer software, for neural
networks
Promotions, 156
Proportionality, assumption of, 47–48
Prybutok, V. R., 91
Psychophysics, 23

QE (quantization error), and solution
quality, 70–71
Quadratic discriminant function, 91–92
Quadratic model, 107n
Quantitative and qualitative methodolo-
gies, integration of, 146–148
Quasi-Newton, 77
Questionnaire survey, 128
Quick propagation, 77
Quinn, R., 128

Rashevsky, Nicolas, 30
RBF (radial basis function), 96
Reanalysis of data, 146
Reed, R., 40
Refinery control systems, 108
Representation, use of term, 32
Representativeness of sample, 52
Research design, 51
for commitment profiles, 127–129
Retraining, 81, 139
Rey, T., 154
Ripley, B., 77
Rizzo, J., 128
RMSE (root mean square error), 63–64,
70, 81
Rosenblatt, Frank, 32–33
Rosenfeld, E., 40
Rumelhart, D., 37–39

Sales revenue, 111–117
Sample data, with unknown distributional characteristics, 14
Sampling error, 52, 109
Sampling theory, 25
Scarborough, D., 74, 96, 111, 154
Schrodt, P., 92
Scientific management, 25
Scientific method, 19–21, 45
Scientific realism, 151
Sederburg, M., 16, 97, 107
Seitz, S. T., 48
Sejnowski, T., 38
Selection models, 58
Self-organizing maps (SOMs), 36–37, 41–42, 56, 64, 68–71, 155–156
    and k-means clustering, 129–133
    Kohonen, 37
    in organizational research, 123–126
    training of, 69–70
Self-organizing systems, 56
Semilinear function, 79–80
Sensitivity analyses, 52, 81, 140, 143, 152–153
Shekhar, S., 90–91
Sigmoid function (semilinear or squashing function), 79–80
Signal processing, 108
Significance testing, 25
Simulated annealing, 77
Singleton, J. C., 91
Size, of SOM, 68–69
Smith, P., 16, 97, 107
Social science, use of term, 24–25
Social sciences
    and neural network applications, 89–90
    use of models, 21
Software. See Computer software, for neural networks; Computer software programs
Solution quality, 70–71, 80–81
Somers, M. J., 47–48, 54–55, 95–96, 128, 148–150
SOMs. See Self-organizing maps (SOMs)
Spencer, Herbert, 30
Spin glasses, 37
Squashing function, 79–80
Staines, G., 128
Standardization of variables, 74
Stanton, J., 16, 97, 107

Starbuck, W. H., 47–48
Statistical models
    of criterion validity, 103–104
    and object of inference, 23–24
Statistical procedures, development of, 25–26
Statistical software, and integration of neural network software, 65–66. See also Computer software
Statistics, ANNs and, 90–94, 141
Statistics, role in social science, 24
StatSoft, Inc., 42
Step transfer function, 31
Stepwise regression model, 94–95, 98
Stigler, Stephen, 24
Stochastic approximation algorithm, 40, 90
Structural equation modeling (SEM), 57, 67, 154
Sturt, G., 20
Succession planning, 156
Summary matrix, 97
Supercomputers, 27
Surface response graphs, 38, 112–113, 115–116, 152–153
Surfaces, nonlinear, 49
Surkan, A. J., 91
Symbolic approach to AI, 28
Synergistic interaction effect, 114
Systemic contamination, and data mining, 108–109

Taxonomy, of neural networks, 40–42, 153–154
    backpropagation, 38–40, 64, 80, 90–92, 99, 112, 119
    Bayesian, 54, 150
    for employee selection, 110–122
    feed-forward, 40, 42–43, 71–81, 155–156
    functional link, 99–100
    learning vector quantization, 71, 95–96
    MLPs, 71
    multiple-layer, 40
    radial basis function, 42, 71
    single-layer, 36, 40
    supervised, 36, 40, 67, 71–81
    unsupervised, 67–71
Taylor, Frederick, 25

Temperature, 77
Test data set, 110
Theory, scientific, 21
Theory development, 45–56, 149–152
Theory testing and refinement, 15
Thissen-Roe, A., 154
Time-bound effects, 109
Topological map, 37
Training, of neural networks, 39, 63–64,
    74–80, 110, 129, 138–140, 142,
    147
  parameters for, 75–80
Training algorithms, 40
Training cycles, 69–70, 138
Training data set, 110
Training iterations, 98–99
Training regime, 77–78
Training schedule, 77
Training term (T$_i$), 36
Training time, 73
Transactions on Neural Networks, 40
Transfer functions, types of, 78–80
Trends, in organizational research using
    ANNs, 146–153
Tuning, 43

Undertraining, 69–70
Uninterpretability of data, 81
United States Ballistics Research Lab, 26
United States Naval Academy, 97–98
United States War Department, 26
Uniterpretability of results, 52
University of Chicago, 30
Utility analysis, 25

Validation model development, 103–104
Validity coefficient, 103

Variables. *See also* Linearity; Nonlinear-
    ity; Theory development
  number, 150–152
  relationships among, 51–56, 62–63,
    84–85, 142, 149
  standardization, 74
  used in employee selection research,
    102n
  used to define commitment profiles,
    128
Variance, unexplained, 106
Visualization. *See* Graphical analysis
Visualization tools, for training ANNs,
    63–65
Voice and image recognition, 108
von Altrock, C., 155

Walker, I., 92–93
Wang, P., 155
Washington State Child Protective
    Services, 95
*Webster's Third New International Diction-
    ary of the English Language,* 24–25
Weinberg, K., 128
Werbos, Paul, 38
Widrow, Bernard, 33–36
Williams, R., 37
Wire frame graphs, 38, 49, 52, 54, 152
"Wizards," in neural network software
    packages, 67

Xerox Corporation, 27
Yerkes, Robert, 25
Yule, George, 23

Zadeh, Lofti, 154

ABOUT THE AUTHORS

David Scarborough holds an MBA and a PhD in human resources from the University of North Texas in Denton. Currently, he is chief scientist at Unicru, Inc., a provider of talent management solutions based in Beaverton, Oregon. Dr. Scarborough and his team wrote Unicru's patents and prepared the patent applications for the first commercial use of neural network predictive modeling for employee selection decision support. Prior to joining Unicru, Dr. Scarborough held consulting and research positions with SHL USA, Batrus Hollweg Ph.D.s, Inc., and American Airlines. He is a member of the American Psychological Association, the Academy of Management, the International Neural Networks Society, the Society for Industrial and Organizational Psychology, and the Society for Human Resource Management.

Mark John Somers, PhD, MBA, is a professor of management at New Jersey Institute of Technology (NJIT) and a member of the doctoral faculty in management at Rutgers University. Dr. Somers holds a BS from Tulane University in New Orleans, Louisiana; an MBA from Baruch College in New York, New York; and a PhD in business with a specialization in organizational behavior from the City University of New York, New York. He joined academia from research groups at IBM, DDB Advertising, and Citibank and served as the dean of the NJIT School of Management from 2000 to 2005. Dr. Somers's research interests are in the micro aspects of organizational behavior, including work attitudes, organizational commitment, job performance, employee turnover, and employee socialization. His interest in neural networks stems from the desire to look at old problems in new ways, with an emphasis on nonlinear thinking and methods. Dr. Somers is currently interested in the application of complexity theory to human behavior in organizations.